RESISTANCE MATTERS

ESSAYS ON LOVE AND ACTION

REVISED AND EXPANDED EDITION

T. THORN COYLE

Trade Print ISBN: 978-1-946476-56-2
Large Print Hardback ISBN: 978-1-946476-57-9

Editing:
Dayle Dermatis

Published by PF Publishing,
An imprint of Triple Flame Inc
3439 SE Hawthorne #203
Portland, OR 97214

Printed and bound by IngramSpark.
Australia: Ingram Content Group AU Pty Ltd, Melbourne, Victoria. US: Lightning Source LLC, La Vergne, Tennessee / Allentown, Pennsylvania / Jackson, Tennessee, United States. UK: Lightning Source UK Ltd, Milton Keynes, United Kingdom. Europe: Lightning Source UK Ltd, with facilities in Germany, France, and Spain. The authorized representative in the European Economic Area is Lightning Source France, 1 Av. Johannes Gutenberg, 78310 Maurepas, France. compliance@lightningsource.fr

Don't give up. Life isn't only a state of emergency.

This work we're all engaged in with one another? It's a long haul. It always has been.

Take a moment. Breathe. Refill your well. Then find a way to pour.

Life matters.
    Love matters.
    Resistance matters.

Dedicated to all you freedom fighters, lovers, artists, truth tellers, and ordinary heroes.

With gratitude for my Kickstarter backers—who believed in this project—and my Patreon supporters, who read these essays first.

You are powerful.
I see you.

INTRODUCTION BY THE AUTHOR

As I write this introduction to the 2025 expanded edition of Resistance Matters, we are entering the second month of a fascist presidency run by a group of billionaires.

Executive orders are coming fast and thick, causing distress and confusion. ICE has ramped up operations, arresting and detaining US citizens and immigrants alike. LGBTQ+ communities are in turmoil. Non-government actors have illegally tapped into our social security and other financial systems. People are fighting back, both federal workers and people on the streets.

Things are moving so quickly, there is no telling what the news will bring on any given day, or where things will stand six months to six years from now.

I'm making my own action plans with people I've worked with in the past while helping those in desperate need right now.

A host of people are organizing. Groups that have never stopped doing the work of equity and justice are sending out calls for new people to join.

Here's what I want to say about all of that:

Do what you have capacity for, because none of us can do it all. Social, economic, and climate justice, antifascism, antiracism, LGBTQIA+ support, and all the rest are important work. Find what you can do and do that thing.

I repeat this refrain throughout many of the essays in this book which were written over the course of a decade. They represent only a fraction of the many I've penned about my relationship to social justice issues over many years.

This book is filled with my personal thoughts, feelings, and experiences, with some resources at the end. These essays were written out of anger, love, and hope. They were written in solidarity, laughter, frustration, grief, and pain. They were written because in order to build the future that is healthy for us all, we need to look at what the past has wrought, and how the present operates.

Simple. Yet hard.

These essays were also written from a place of gratitude.

I thank all the activists I know. And the teachers, parents, artists, gardeners, and singers. I thank everyone who works so hard to make this world a vibrant, loving place to live.

My hope is that some of these essays might expand your understanding of what others are going through, and that other essays will inspire you to look at your own life and figure out what help you can offer at this point in time.

Unless you have a solid, trusted crew, don't think in grand, dramatic gestures. Think in small actions and solidarity.

Take lessons from the folks who have lived under the thumb of oppression for decades or centuries.

Uplift and support those most affected.

Use what privilege you have to intervene when necessary, or to make helpful connections.

Move. Act. Take a break. Rest. Find joy. Then move and act again.

Don't comply.

Don't give up.

In love and solidarity —

T. Thorn Coyle

18 February 2025

CONTENTS

PART 4

ON WHITE SUPREMACY

PART 5

WE'RE HERE, WE'RE QUEER

PART 6

THE LONG HAUL

PART 7

ON JOY AND MUTUAL AID

PART 1

SOMETIMES RESISTANCE…

ONE
RESISTANCE MATTERS

The only hopelessness is in giving up.

The only hopelessness is in saying we are defeated.

The only hopelessness is in the refusal to take back and claim our power.

You are powerful. I see you.

You are beautiful. I see you.

You are terrified. I see you.

You weep, and wail, and take to your bed, and take the streets and hug and rail.

And then you take a breath.

And you take some time.

And you find all of the things that help you not despair, or not get stuck in eternal rage.

And you ask yourself, "What are my skills?"

And you ask yourself, "What are my talents?"

And you ask yourself, "What do I need to learn?"

And you ask yourself, "How can I be of service, in this moment, to this time?"

And then you look around and ask, "Where can I plug in?" or "How can I help organize?"

Use what you have—time, energy, and skill—and figure out three possible ways to offer that.

Do some research. Ponder.

Then pick one of those three things. *Any* thing. Not the perfect thing. Not the exact right thing. Pick one thing and try it for a while. And learn how to control your ego so you don't step back so far you disappear and you don't step so far forward that everything becomes about your needs and your ideas. There are many practices that help with that. If you don't already have one, find one. Meditation. Martial arts. Prayer.

And pay attention.

Black and brown and Native and trans and queer people have been telling the rest of us: these systems do not serve us, nor do they make us safe. Those of us who have not paid attention before? We need to say, "I'm so sorry I didn't hear or see or comprehend you. I'm going to literally throw cold water in my face each morning and remind myself to pay attention now." And, "I will educate myself from the rich writings and resources available in my communities or in the library and the Internet."

Then we figure out how we can actively be of service to those who need us most (and sometimes that includes ourselves and our families). And we commit to it.

We figure out what solidarity means. Then work on making that possible.

People need food.

People need beauty.

People need skills.

People need care and protection.

People need to find ways to show up.

How can you help? How can we help?

Black resistance matters. Native resistance matters. Latinx resistance matters. Asian resistance matters. Trans resistance matters. Queer resistance matters. Immigrant resistance matters. Muslim resistance matters...

Your resistance matters.

Organizing matters.

What do you want to build? Figure it out. Ask your friends. Pray. Strategize. Train.

Act.

Include longevity in your strategies. How do we build in self care, and rest, and breaks, and laughter, and music, and paying the bills, and sharing food and art? How do we get and remain as healthy as our particular bodies and psyches and families can be?

How do we say to our comrades, "I need a break, can you shoulder this for the week?"

How do we say to our cohort, "This feels like a problem, can we talk about it and figure it out?"

How do we say, "I've got energy right now, let me be useful." Or, "I've got these skills to share."

Movements sometimes get crushed and sometimes fail. They fail because of burnout or ego clash or other life events crashing in.

They do not have to fail or fizzle. And when attempts to crush them come—as they always do—we can recognize them and re-organize.

We can create interlocking avenues of support and

resistance. We can create interlocking avenues to build what we desire.

So, after the initial assessment of "What can I do and how do I plug in?" we all must ask, "How do we build a living, flexible system that can grow and change with us, over time?"

It won't be easy. But the alternative is to sink back into complacency, or hopelessness, or disinterest, or despair.

Please don't do that. Keep finding ways to re-engage.

Don't look for a savior. Don't look to be a savior.

We need every one of us to do this. And those of us in relative positions of privilege need to listen to those who have been more marginalized. They have the most necessary input of all: how to live, survive, and thrive under systems that are hell-bent on crushing individuals and communities. And how to continue to love, even in the midst of that.

We need love right now. We need resilience. We need wisdom from avenues we've never even thought to seek it from.

We need each other.

Please stick around.

November 2016

TWO
TOO MUCH TO SAY

My social justice awakening began seriously at age thirteen, when, to my shock, I discovered the adults I interviewed for a school project all supported the death penalty. I began marching and blockading and engaging in minor acts of political vandalism at age sixteen. I have never stopped considering matters of justice and injustice since, while doing my best to work for the former.

These past few years, I'm not out on the streets much, because of the aftermath of a brain injury coupled with an autoimmune disorder that sometimes slows me down. Instead, I write fiction that mixes my radical sensibilities with magic. I write poetry and engage in small actions, trying to help the people working on the ground, wherever they are. I talk with friends.

And right now? There seems to be a battle on every front. There always seems to be too much to say. About too many things.

I wish we could sit in a circle, with cups of tea, and share our stories, bridging the divide sown by misinformation, terror, and fear. But we can't, so I write these words instead.

There are psychopaths in the world, and not the benign kind—which do exist—but the kind that crave money, power over others, violence, and control.

There are also too many people who carry water for these severely unbalanced human beings, profiting from the actions of those who have no use for empathy or compassion. Most people would rather work together on some level, and be kind. Yet collectively, we have allowed the cold and calculating, power-hungry ones to rule us all. The lovers of authoritarianism feel safer that way.

The dangerous ones and their water carriers enslave others. They use rape as a tool of war. They control bodily autonomy. They try to purge anyone who stands against them. They take hostages. They slaughter tens of thousands: in Sudan, Congo, and Palestine.

They strive to pit ordinary people against one another. They tell us to fear those they deem not like us. They tell us being gay or trans is a crime. They tell us having a uterus is license to give up personal sovereignty. They tell us that to arrive as an immigrant or refugee is to be subhuman. They send children into mines, blazing fields, and meat packing plants. They tell us that being Indigenous means to deserve less than nothing. They say that being Black or brown is a sign of suspicion, and sometimes a mark of sudden death. They tell us being impoverished is our fault. They say that the ultra-wealthy are rightfully blessed. They tell us to shut up, roll over, and get back to work.

They cling to wealth and righteousness, to shareholders and war.

Sometimes there is too much to say, but I can say this:

We don't need to follow their game plan. We can resist. We don't need to pit ourselves against each other. We can seek deeper conversation instead. We can think. We can act. We can eschew the shackles of xenophobia and hate. We can look to the bees, pollinating the next season, working together to create sweetness.

We can claim our own collective power.

We can each take one action—large or small—and grow a little braver for each other and ourselves. We can imagine pathways toward joy, pleasure, and liberation.

In this way, we shall build a more just world.

May, 2024

THREE
SOMETIMES RESISTANCE

Sometimes resistance means blocking the buses rounding up immigrants.

Sometimes resistance means filming the police.

Sometimes resistance means loudly pointing out what is happening.

Sometimes resistance means stockpiling birth control for redistribution.

Sometimes resistance means offering a warm blanket.

Sometimes resistance means walking someone through government bureaucracy.

Sometimes resistance means planting a community garden in an empty lot.

Sometimes resistance means supporting Drag Time Story Hour.

Sometimes resistance means setting up a free food pantry in your neighborhood.

Sometimes resistance means not complying with unethical orders.

Sometimes resistance means offering a spare bed to a trans teen.

Sometimes resistance means gathering your union buddies and comrades to face down fascists marching through your town.

Sometimes resistance means showing up to a city council meeting to protest camp sweeps.

Sometimes resistance means sitting in an old growth tree.

Sometimes resistance means running for the school board.

Sometimes resistance means staffing a crisis hotline.

Sometimes resistance means supporting libraries against budget cuts and censorship.

Sometimes resistance means standing by neighbors in the park when they're told they can't gather.

Sometimes resistance means protecting a health clinic.

Sometimes resistance means protecting a watershed.

Sometimes resistance means striking for better pay and working conditions.

Sometimes resistance means being fully who you are.

January, 2025

FOUR
A MANIFESTO

Our societies don't have to be this messed up.

We can learn from past mistakes.

We can stop operating out of sheer ego-protection and fear.

We can choose to not preference the making of money over the well-being of community.

We. Can. Do. This.

We all play a part in upholding the churning of oppressive systems, especially those of us in the middle and upper economic classes. Especially those of us who are able bodied and neurotypical. Especially those of us with white skin.

We consistently place too great of a burden on the poor, disenfranchised, and otherwise marginalized people.

Those of us who live relatively comfortable lives must choose to give up some measure of our comfort. We must choose to actively lobby for a world that will better serve

– rather than punish – communities that are currently at risk and under pressure.

We can topple the towers of government and greed.

How?

By taking the power from those who have it.

By holding corporations accountable.

By firing every single person in government who is not acting in the interests of the well being of this planet and all the beings on it.

By insisting that shareholder's interests are less important than healthy communities.

By insisting that those who are most adversely affected by our current systems be given some of the benefits of these systems as an interim step toward changing those systems.

By asking counsel from those most adversely affected by our current systems on how to both dismantle these systems and create systems that foster greater strength, longevity, and support for all.

By offering fair exchange of whatever the current currency is within those systems to those most adversely affected, as payment for their insight and time.

We can foment revolution. And by revolution, I mean a complete overhaul of how our society is currently structured, root to branch.

We can:

Educate ourselves on the horrors of the prison industrial complex and the realities of policing.

Lobby for the abolition of police and prisons.

Listen to and amplify the voices of those most affected by these systems.

Brainstorm with as broad a coalition as possible on varied solutions for true community safety, mental and emotional health, and economic security.

We can:

Remember that collectively, we have power.

Working as individuals, on individual actions, is one small part of the picture, but must be seen as a strategy in the service of joining our personal power with the power of the group.

Remember that working together, our power increases.

Share skills, ideas, food, and laughter.

We can:

Insist that making money not be the driving force behind all business choices.

Insist that community well-being, and the well-being of air, water, soil, and all the creatures of the earth be paramount.

We can:

Work to dismantle our current interlocking systems of oppression, knowing that this will take time.

Simultaneously, use what power and resources we have within these current systems to ease suffering and inequity, while remaining conscious that this is not a long-term solution.

Remember that stop-gaps and bandages are sometimes necessary to treat the proximate – and very real– symptoms of our current damaging systems.

We can:

Stop giving our power away to those we currently name as being "in power" but who only further erode community well-being. This is not power. This is manipulation and oppression.

Choose to give power, strength, and backing to community organizers, and to groups working toward community safety and community well-being.

Choose to give power and backing to to those who serve to create art, and beauty, and health, and teaching, and resource sharing.

We can:

Involve ourselves to the best of our abilities with groups –however imperfect– who are doing the work of fostering community health and well-being, or who are actively working to dismantle current, oppressive systems.

We can:

Remember that working organically takes time.

Remember that taking time means also taking care of our own needs as well as being attentive to the needs of others.

Share resources.

We can:

Remember that there is always room to celebrate joy.

Remember that, in fact, what we are building toward is greater joy, and therefore, supporting anything that fosters joy is part of the revolution.

We can:

Pick ourselves up when we fall.

Apologize.

Listen.

Raise each other up.

Ask for help.

Offer help.

We can:

Re-evaluate our values.

Learn to love one another and ourselves better and better.

Revolution is possible. Every single day.

October, 2017

PART 2

CARING FOR EACH OTHER

FIVE
IN NEED OF BEAUTY

Right now, I feel tired. Not tired of everything, mind you. But tired of important topics. Tired of news cycles. Tired of in-fighting. Tired of politics. Tired of hustle. Tired of fascism. Tired of inequity. Tired of police killings. Tired of murders. Tired of oppression. Tired of racism. Tired of sexism. Tired of transmisogyny. Tired of the litanies of hopelessness, hatred, and fear that scroll across my Facebook and Twitter feeds.

I need a break from it. Just for a small while.

I want to listen to the birds, and the rustle of the trees, and the cars going on their way. I want to ask the squirrel why it is so upset today. What in the world is it chuck-chucking at?

I want to feel the spring air.

My friend, the musician Sharon Knight, reminds us that beauty and lifting one another up are choices.

In a world that is trying to grind us all down, I want to take refuge in beauty.

This doesn't mean that I'll forget my suffering brothers, sisters, and siblings. It just means that I'll refill the well of my soul for awhile, before re-entering the fray.

We need this. We all need this. Especially those of us who work hard for others every day. And even those of us who don't.

What in you is longing for a rest? A break? Some beauty?

Can you take an hour or so and fill the well of your heart, mind, body, and soul?

I invite us all to pause today. Find a piece of art to look at. Listen to some music. Dance. Go for a walk. Laugh. Brush your hand against a tree. Smell the ocean. Find one flower. Kiss a friend. Watch the sky. Read something that gives you pleasure.

Easy as it is to forget sometimes, the world is not only hustle or suffering.

The world is filled with beauty. Sometimes it is small, and hard to catch. But it is there. In someone's face. In the way the sun hits a building. Even in the most squalid, depressed conditions, beauty finds a way.

I hope that today, beauty finds its way to you. And that you rest in it awhile.

May 2016

SIX

IN PRAISE OF KINDNESS

I'm not always the *nicest* person.

I'm impatient, and as an introvert (yeah, despite my "extroverted" presentation), I can sometimes lack generosity in my attempts to parse out energy, attention, and time.

Not being naturally *nice* makes it even more important for me to attempt to practice being *kind.*

I do this by recalling the sort of person I want to be.

I do this by recalling the world I seek to build. The world I want to live in.

Do I want to live in a world run by greed, anger, oppression, and tearing one another down? No.

Therefore, I must practice, daily, living in the sort of world I want. Even though it may not exist in the doddering, top-heavy, inequitable society I currently live in, I can sow as many seeds of a new world as possible, from the smallest interactions to my attitude.

Even when I feel like I fail, I can always try again.

And in the midst of my failures and missteps? I'm so grateful when people choose to be kind to me.

KINDNESS: The acknowledgement that we are "of a kind" or perhaps even "akin" to one another.

The Old English root of kind meant "with the feeling of relatives for each other."

Therefore: To seek kindness is to acknowledge, "You and I, despite our differences, are related. We are not completely separate from one another."

To seek kindness is to seek connection.

To seek kindness is to empathize with someone else, no matter how much we may dislike them, or how foreign they may seem.

What can we relate to? Recollection of relation is a step toward kindness.

KINDNESS—NOT niceness—can require firmness. Sometimes kindness even requires our anger, or the sort of truth telling that makes others feel uncomfortable.

Sometimes kindness means confrontation.

Sometimes kindness means holding someone's hand.

Sometimes kindness means walking away before more harm is done.

SO OFTEN, the kind thing is to act firmly, clearly, and state what I need to in as respectful a manner as possible.

Remember, I want to build the world I wish to live in. So I don't want to engage in personal attacks. I don't want to degrade anyone. But I do want to stand firmly in my truth.

Also, kindness is not subjecting ourselves or others to abuse.

I used to work full time in a soup kitchen. Sometimes, in order to respect the space and respect our guests, we chose to kick another guest out for the day.

That was offering respect to the space and to the person we asked to leave. It was saying, "Here's a boundary. We gave you a chance to honor it. You crossed that boundary, so we are asking you to leave until you can work within our community agreements again."

To allow one guest to trample on all the others is not an act of kindness and connection. Rather, it allows one person to rend the threads of connection for everyone, leaving community agreements and safe spaces in tatters.

To allow someone to trample on ourselves is also not a kindness to either of us.

Kindness requires both empathy and boundaries.

Therefore, sometimes kindness means offering someone money, or a meal, or a shoulder to cry on, or a listening ear.

And sometimes kindness means saying, "That's enough."

I WANT to keep trying to practice kindness. Even when I fail.

And I need to recall: sometimes kindness needs to be directed at the self. Empathy and boundaries help us all.

We can't rescue each other, as much as we want to. We can try our best, and sometimes we'll succeed. But we can rescue our inner lives from hatred and vitriol and division.

This helps us to cultivate greater empathy, the knowledge of who we are and where we stand. It reminds us what connection feels like.

We can start by imagining a world where we are kind.

September 2016

SEVEN
THE THINGS THAT HELP

"We best rescue each other in daily heartbeats."
— Scherezade Siobhan

WAR. Tornadoes. Rising temperatures. Displaced people. Mass incarceration. Increased poverty. People sleeping on the streets. Another shooting. Ongoing pandemic...

And then there is us: Trying to live our lives. Pay our bills. Take care of our families and friends, and hopefully, ourselves.

A client recently asked me how to keep going with life when things felt bleak or uncertain. I have my moments, too. As a matter of fact, I recently said out loud during a webinar that what my heart wants is "To forgive myself for not saving the world."

Now, my mind knows that is ego talking. It is arrogant to think I can do any such thing as save the world.

And yet... when the pain of the world grows so large, and the suffering around us so immense, the pain cracks us. It is natural to want to save something.

So what do we do? What do *I* do? I take a breath. I find my center. I remember that I am but one cell in the body of the cosmos and that every cell has a function and a place.

What helps me reconnect to my function and my place?

What helps me keep engaging with a world in pain? A world that feels simultaneously on fire and drowning?

There are five things I revisit on a daily basis:

Meditation.

Mutual Aid.

Creativity.

Learning.

Nature.

MEDITATION IS a continual return to breath, to centering, to stillness. Meditation helps me to return to a sense of being, rather than my frantic wish to do. Meditation offers the reminder that there can be stillness and breath, even if only one minute at a time. Meditation is a reconnection to a world that is not "productive" and hurried. Even if thoughts or emotions race the whole time, meditation helps us to slow down.

Have trouble meditating? That is fine. There are guided meditation apps that help. I've got some videos up on YouTube. And if all else fails? Simply sit and breathe for five minutes. Don't worry if your body aches, your mind races, or your emotions heave. The point is to be with what *is*. Make some space. And then breathe some more.

Mutual Aid is the exchange of resources for mutual benefit. It is the sharing of skills, goods, and help and the reminder that together, we have enough. Do you have extra food? Carpentry or computer skills? Money? An extra bed? Can you connect folks to each other? Drive someone to an appointment? Can you help build a community garden, or tutor kids, stock a pantry, give away books, lend some tools? Can you organize your neighborhood to check on elders? Design a spreadsheet to help other disabled folks during black outs or fires? Provide basic medical training or get some? And conversely, what do you need?

Mutual Aid reminds me that we are interconnected and cannot survive without each other. That, like it or not, we live in interlocking communities. When things feel too big, this reminds me that there are a myriad of small ways to help or be helped. We don't need to wait to be saved.

Creativity is the act of tapping into the flow of life. This includes baking, cooking, building, gardening, singing, dancing, painting, writing... Creativity reminds us that the whole world is constantly in the cycle of creation. Plants are resting in the soil, or sprouting, or blooming outright. Birds and insects are building nests or pollinating.

Creativity is everywhere. On days when it feels as if

the world is filled with nothing but destruction? Put on a favorite piece of music, and dance.

Learning is the process of taking in and assimilating information. I study every day. I watch interviews with professional film makers and read articles by prison abolitionists. I study the craft and business of writing. I study naturalists, woodworkers, activists, and musicians. I listen to friends, colleagues, and family. And I practice, every day: spiritual practice, listening practice, writing practice... Learning keeps me open, curious, and humble.

Learning is another way we share in this world.

Nature is all around us, even in dense cities. Nature reconnects me to all that is and reminds me that everything is interconnected and interdependent. Soil. Rain. Air. Birds. Sky. Flowers. Insects. Trees. I don't wait to get out into the woods, or desert, or ocean. Connecting with the natural world on my daily walks through the city is a key part of what supports me in being healthy, happy, and whole.

So, how often do you connect with plants, animals, water, or trees? How often do you pause to enjoy the sky or the sound of birds?

ALL FIVE OF these practices are touchstones and reminders that there is beauty in the world. There are humans, animals, and insects creating amazingly glorious things. There is music in the air and earth beneath my feet. And in the sky are planets, stars, and a large, bright moon.

And in my chest is a heartbeat, same as yours. Our

heartbeats tell us we are alive, together, on this glorious spinning world. We breathe together with all that lives.

We conspire, even in the midst of suffering, to reconnect with this varied and marvelous world.

March 2022

EIGHT
TO RUN IN, FREEZE, OR FLEE

Please be patient while I lay out some things that may seem disparate or self-indulgent at first. They do connect:

SELF-PRESERVATION IS IMPORTANT. We need our bodies, souls, and minds together, functioning, and as healthy as can be.

Self-preservation is also not enough.

One of my writing teachers, in talking about fictional characters, outlines three basic human types: Those who run in. Those who freeze. Those who call for help. I might add a fourth: Those who run away.

These types are believed to be hardwired into us. We need to know our basic type to better train to compensate the weaknesses each type has.

I'm a runner inner. A fighter. I can't help it. However, I've learned to moderate this for reasons of self-preservation. I had to learn to do so at a very young age in order to manage my encounters with a randomly violent father.

My impulse to run in would have been dangerous for me, so I taught myself to freeze, railing at the injustice of it inside, wanting to punch things because forcing my runner-inner self to freeze bottled up a lot of anger.

I've run toward situations and intervened numerous times when people were later aghast that I did so: confronting a man when he was trying to keep his elderly mother from getting in a car. Coming right up to a woman who was being held by her partner, not allowed to get on the train, to ask her point blank if she needed help. Stopping a boy from choking another boy over a wad of drug money.

Over and over, I've done this. It's not noble. Sometimes it's probably stupid. *It's just my impulse.*

At the soup kitchen, I ran in to break up fights, often interposing my body between people in order to attempt to keep the peace. The interventions worked, though I got clipped a couple of times, and threatened with violence more than once. I ran in to break up fights until one day it became too much for my emotional body. I needed to take a break, for my long term self-preservation.

At a Trans Pride March, I heard shouts for security, and immediately started moving toward the noise. I didn't think. I just moved. Luckily, I wasn't needed.

At a march and rally for Black Lives to counter multiple extrajudicial killings by police, I was standing on the edge of the second rally site, taking photos and live tweeting some of the speakers. In the middle of one tweet, I saw some people backing a white man up around 15 feet from me. I saw him reach to his waist and unsnap a holster. *Shit. He's about to pull a gun!* I thought.

There were some children nearby. I turned and starting backing them up, away from the direction the man was heading. Once other adults came to take the children out, I turned, to see what to do.

This story is here because of what I did next:

I started to walk around one of the cars, looking for a sight line. I thought *Is there any way I could get to him from the side or behind and get the gun?* No. There wasn't. And other people were much closer to the man.

He was waving the gun around, and the shout came up to "Hit the ground!" So I made a decision. I could do nothing at that point, so I crouched down for a moment, generally shielded, a few feet behind a car. The rapid-fire thoughts going through my head were the equivalent of *There isn't anything I can do to help this situation so the prudent thing to do is to get myself out of harm's way.* I had to tell myself that.

I had to remind myself that sometimes, when a person is waving a gun around, it's good to temporarily crouch near a car.

Self-preservation is a good thing.

All of this is said in service to these times.

I know a lot of activists and organizers. I also know a lot of people just trying to get through, day to day. Black parents. Trans women. Many other people who just don't know when danger will turn the corner.

I want to speak out loud something many Black women activists have been saying lately, because it is so necessary: Take care of yourselves. Whatever that means. Whether it means going to the gym. Or not reading the news. Or sitting in a garden instead of doing whatever else is on your list. Take whatever kind of break you need to. And push yourself to allow that break.

Especially if it goes against your natural impulses.

I want to equally speak out loud something on the other side: Some of us err too much on the side of self-preservation. PEOPLE ARE DYING IN THE STREETS RIGHT NOW. And they have been for far too long. Some communities have been reeling from it, and built around the pain. For the last several years, those of us who could ignore it before have known about it directly.

So if your impulse is to always just tend your own garden, and to mind your own business, now is the time to step outside. Now is the time to speak up. Now is the time to get in your friend's and neighbor's business and say, "Hey, that is not okay with me."

And maybe it is time to march. And maybe it is time to organize with a group that's already putting in the work towards social, racial, or economic justice. Or to protect women and children. Or the water supply. Or to keep oligarchs and plutocrats from stealing any more than they already have. There are many groups doing the work. We can all find one that speaks to us. Organization is important. We need each other. We can't get caught up with in-fighting, but must keep our eyes on the larger aim.

We can also try other actions: Tell a growing list of corporations, "Prison labor is theft, oppression, and a form of slavery, plus it undermines local jobs. Stop doing this." Start a letter campaign to Congress. Harass your city council about policing issues. Call the chief of police.

Sit in, or blockade. Say something when a person on the bus is harassing an immigrant or a woman.

Know your impulse type, and gently practice countering it in order to increase options and become more effective for the long run:

If your impulse is to freeze, practice the small things first. Practice calling for help. Ask, "Did you see that? What should we do?"

If your impulse is to call for help, practice the small things first. Practice moving toward something that feels slightly risky, like countering a racist or misogynist or anti-queer statement with the words, "Did you just hear what you said, friend? That's pretty dehumanizing."

If your impulse is to run in, practice the small things first. Ask if you've been running in too much. Ask what you can do that is at the very least the equivalent of letting yourself crouch behind a car if there is nothing effective running in will do.

If your impulse is to run away, practice the small things first. Stand still and face the situation. Look at it. Then run if you still need to. But you might also find a way to call for help, or to offer help yourself.

For us all, no matter what our impulses, I hope we ask for help from friends, colleagues, and family. Say, "I'm trying to speak up more. Will you be a safe space for me to collapse afterward, if I need to?" Or say, "I know I'm doing too much, but I don't know how to stop. Will you call me up to take a walk once a week?" Or say, "I don't even know where to begin. How are you coping? What ways are you finding to help? Is there a group you recommend we connect with?"

We are all needed, in so many situations right now, and we are needed for the long journey ahead.

Please choose self-preservation, but simultaneously, please choose to offer the help that is so desperately needed right now.

The world has a need, and you have a need. It's time to figure out the places they can meet.

June 2016

NINE
THE ICE OF CHANGE
ON RUNES, SOLIDARITY, AND NOT BEING OKAY

"what didn't you do to bury me
but you forgot that I was a seed"
— Dinos Christianopoulos, 1978

"They tried to bury us, they didn't know we were seeds."
— Mexican Activists, 2013

It's okay to not be okay.

I know I'm not the first person to type or say these words, but this week? I'm repeating them for myself.

Times are rough. Really rough. Folks are freezing in detention camps, on the streets, and in their homes. People don't have enough food. The pandemic still holds us in its grip.

We all know these are perilous times. Well, except perhaps for those insulated by so much wealth they can avoid seeing anything beyond the golden latches on their doors or their trips to Cancun.

That said, together, we've done our best. We've done well. We've helped each other. We've made countless pots of soup. We've wiped noses. We've figured out how to work online, or get through endless holds with unemployment. We've kept our children fed, somehow. Gotten some exercise. Binged some television. Maybe even read a book or three.

But dealing with rolling wave of disaster after disaster with no end apparent?

It's hard, my friends. And I'm feeling that this week.

One morning, after meditation and prayer, I pulled a rune. I wanted insight. Some advice, maybe.

Carved into the wood, was a sort of H shape. Hagalaz. The hail stone.

"Shit," I said, as a first reaction. "Thanks."

While that "thanks" was tinged with a sarcastic "thanks a lot" it also led me to ponder what pulling that rune might mean.

We are, of course, in the midst of massive ice and snow storms in much of the American continent. The rune is partially a reflection of that.

But Hagalaz not only signals the ice of destruction that lays waste to crops...

Hagalaz is not only "the sickness of serpents"...

Hagalaz is also "the coldest of grains" and a reminder that the ice will melt, and water the fields, so something new can grow. In its other form, which looks like a cross hatched, simple snowflake, it is said to hold the seed of creation within the heart of destruction.

I often relate Hagalaz to the Tower in Tarot. Some have said we've been living in the Tower for a long time.

The old ways are crumbling, struck by lightning. We tumble through the air, not certain when, or if, we will ever land.

> "We can bring to birth a new world from the ashes of the old." — Solidarity Forever

---

THIS WEEK'S reminder of the seed of creation embedded in the center of destruction reminds me that:

Within ourselves, we have the power to destroy.

Within ourselves, we have the power to create.

We are—right now, if we choose it—seeding the possibility of a better new world that can and will grow from the charred and soggy rubble of the old.

Every action we take that says we still believe in one another...

Every poem written and song sung...

Every time we say "no" to the machinery of greed and oppression...

Every meal shared...

Every hard conversation had...

Every defiant facing off with eyes mirrored behind shields and visors, tasers and guns...

Every dream and vision spoken out loud...

Everything we love and act to protect...

ALL OF THESE ARE SEEDS.

SO YES, these are the worst times I've lived through—and I've survived some very bad times, and acknowledge that others have not survived. But the bad times I've lived through? They were all leading up to this. They were all part of the long, slow, shaking of the Tower crumbling, and the hailstones hitting.

And all these years, those I love have been frantically planting seeds.

Times are bad. It's okay to not be okay. But please know, that even in your worst struggling, and even on the days you might give up, seeds are being planted, everywhere.

You are not alone.

We are all planting and germinating, and nurturing together.

February, 2021

TEN
THE PRICE OF A CUP OF COFFEE:
ON PRIVILEGES AND RIGHTS

I walked home from a local café, carrying a reused and recycled cup tray filled with our weekly treat. Three mochas, one caffeinated, two decaf, all of them made with oat milk. The treat is one way we try to keep our local independent businesses afloat during this time of closures and pandemic. And sometimes I like to have a destination to walk to.

When I exited the main drag, I pulled my face mask down as I walked on the sidewalk beneath the trees, and past dogs guarding their homes. One block later, I saw someone heading my direction. They walked in the street, dressed in too many layers, lugging a rolling suitcase.

As I always do when approaching another person, I pulled my mask back on.

The person noticed, and began to speak.

"That's right. I hope you die from your damn Covid. You and your damn Starbucks coffee."

I kept walking, and she kept walking too, me on the

sidewalk, her in the middle of the street. She kept ranting at me, in an accusing tone. One of the things I think I caught her say after I passed was that she didn't have any coffee.

It was one of those moments where, if I thought for a moment the hot beverage wouldn't have been thrown in my face, I would've offered her one of the three that I carried back to my household.

But besides the lack of assurance that she would accept such a gift, we had already passed each other and it would have felt confrontational to turn back.

So, I kept going on home and she headed to wherever it was she was going.

But I doubt it was a place with running water, indoor plumbing, and warm beds.

I did hope she had some shelter, and a way to stay warm.

I'VE BEEN THINKING a lot lately about rights and privileges, and the way we tend to conflate the terms. My weekly purchase of three oat milk mochas from my local independent café is a privilege I enjoy.

The nice home I share with my chosen family is another privilege I enjoy. The type of food I eat? That's a privilege, too.

However, food, water, and shelter themselves are not privileges. They are rights. And saying I am privileged to have them at all, means we run the risk of beginning to believe that not everyone has the right to nourishing food, clean water to drink, and a stable place to live and to call home.

The thing I'm pointing to here, is that too many people don't even have basic rights.

Case in point: another local shop owner commented recently that at age forty-three he was voting for the first time.

Voting is a right he had not been afforded before, because the state had seen fit to keep him caged for I'm not sure how many years. No matter what we think of the system—and no matter what we think of voting—in the United States at least, it's supposed to be a right, not a privilege.

We blur these concepts too often, to our detriment. We call things privileges that are rights, and we call things rights that are really privileges. And those with the most privilege? Too often they believe they are the only ones who should have any rights at all.

I have a lot more rights than the person cursing my face mask and fancy coffee on the street. I have a lot more privileges, too.

I don't feel comfortable with either, nor should I.

I don't work any harder than that person does. It takes a lot of effort to find food and shelter when they aren't givens. It takes a lot more effort to stay safe in a society that would rather not see you at all, and when you are seen, mostly it is to be kicked in one way or another.

I'm no better or more deserving than the person lugging a wheeled case behind them, ranting.

So why is my life easier?

Because I am fortunate. Sheer circumstance, chance,

effort, talent, and luck, all combined and I ended up with chosen family. With a house. With food. With clear water.

And my chance of getting gunned down by police? They're pretty slim.

I have privileges, and therefore, I need to put in more effort to make sure that others get their rights.

October, 2020

ELEVEN
SOLIDARITY BECOMES OUR RESISTANCE

On a domestic US flight—from SFO to JFK—federal agents checked every passenger's identification before allowing them to exit the airplane. They said they were seeking a non-documented immigrant.

People complied. Now, I wasn't there, so perhaps some of them questioned what was happening, but as far as I know, every person showed their ID. The "immigrant" was not found.

What if every single person on that airplane said as loudly as possible, right to the agents' faces, "There is no reason for you to ask for identification. There is nothing that compels me to offer you proof of who I am. In solidarity with any immigrants who may or may not be on this airplane, I refuse to comply."

Imagine it. All it takes is for one person to take a breath and begin.

We can practice saying those words out loud: "I refuse to comply."

There's a lot of talk about "resistance" these days. A

lot of complaining about the current state of the US government.

People are showing up in solidarity: at airports, at courthouses, on the streets, on the plains of North Dakota. However, even if they were only coordinated hours before, these are all planned protests.

Planned protests are good, and are often necessary civic engagement. I support planned protests, and civil disobedience as well.

But I want to talk about what solidarity looks like on the fly. I want to talk about what is necessary right now—and has been ignored by some of us for too long—which is for all of us to prepare ourselves to be fucking brave in the fucking moment. To not comply with authority in order to better protect those among us who may be at higher risk.

The systems in place? For many of us, they may feel like minor annoyances. Inconveniences. What they really are is part of a machine that is deadly to many communities.

For years, as a frequent business flier, I refused to use the scanners, wanting to make the TSA's job harder. I was always polite to individual agents, but I did not want to be pleasant to the machine. Finally, after several years of this, one early morning I just could not bear to be groped anymore. So I walked into the scanner and raised my arms.

Lack of solidarity had finally worn me down. That's what the machine of empire wants.

The only time in the last three years that I refused the scanner was while traveling with a trans femme friend.* The odds of her getting searched no matter what were high, so in solidarity, I submitted to the groping. Too little, for sure. It was an act of good faith, nothing more.

But what if hundreds of thousands of people in the airport said, "No. This is ridiculous. Why are we all under suspicion? We refuse to play your game anymore."? What if one million refused? Three million? What would happen then?

The machine would be given pause. It would either falter and grind to a halt, or it would turn the crank harder, increasing the threat from inconvenience to actual blatant oppression.

And more of us would see the machine then, for what it really is.

We might see the same oppression that more marginalized people—Black Americans, Mexican Americans, disabled Americans, Native Americans, poor Americans, trans Americans, immigrant Americans—have been telling us for years they have been living, struggling, and, far too often, dying under.

The machines so many of us think are there to keep us safe? They aren't. They are there to prove their control over us all, to offer some of us perks and privileges—private property protection is an attractive goad to compliance—and to remind those whom they torture that no one will stand up for them. Ever. That solidarity is a whim at best, and at worst, it is a lie.

Last week, an off-duty white police officer assaulted a thirteen-year-old boy. When the boy's friends finally tried to intervene, the white man pulled a gun. In the video footage, among the sea of young brown people, it is clear that at least one other white adult male was there, witnessing the scene. He did nothing to help the young teens.

Solidarity requires standing up to people who claim authoritarian control of every kind, most often when it is being used against people who may not look or sound like us. Remember: it is bullying, even when it smiles.

Solidarity requires those of us with any kind of social privilege to stand up for those with less social privilege.

On a train once, there was a friendly, developmentally disabled Black man, singing. At one stop, police came on board and asked him to step off the car.

"Why?" I loudly said. "He wasn't doing anything!"

Other people chimed in, too, saying similar things.

The police tried to wave us off, and calm us down, meanwhile insisting the man exit the train. I finally stood up, saying loudly to the police, "He wasn't doing anything wrong!"

Some other passengers stood up, too. Backup. The thing we always hope will happen, but which doesn't always.

Meanwhile, the man, clearly frightened, was frantically giving his phone number to another person, so she could call his mother and tell her why he wasn't going to show up. She would worry if he was late.

All of us kept repeating, "He didn't do anything wrong! Leave him alone!"

If the police took this person off the train, they were taking me, too, and maybe some others, and I positioned my body so that this was made clear.

The police finally backed off and left. The doors closed. The train continued on its way.

Solidarity saved that man from who knows what fate. I've heard the personal stories of people falsely accused, dragged from trains, slammed onto platforms, beaten in jails.

One man, at least, was saved from that treatment on that one day. He was able to visit his mother instead.

That is what solidarity looks like: a group of random people deciding to say "enough!" to authoritarianism. A group of random people momentarily suspending their own need for comfort or safety in order to help someone in need.

All it took was one person to start it, and for others to feel brave enough to follow through.

If our idea of resistance does not include these common, very tangible acts of solidarity, I'm not sure what exactly we are resisting.

We are most likely resisting an idea behind computer screens, from the comfort of our homes.

There is a long history of solidarity via direct action. We can take inspiration from the many stories of people who'd had enough.

Let's learn from the past to build the future.

Let's use our voices, our bodies, and our minds.

Let's show up for those who've been shouting without enough back up for far too long.

Let's resist this shit for real.

February, 2017

Author's note: I write this for the many middle class, able-bodied white people who may be new to the idea of active resistance. Everyone else? I see you. I know you've been resisting in a lot of ways, large and small, for a very, very, long time. Thank you.

**And yes, things are about to get much worse for trans people in the US right now.*

TWELVE
ON THE POWER OF SPEAKING UP
FOR JORDAN NEELY

Several years ago, I was riding the BART train one afternoon, sitting and reading a book. A Black man in a jaunty hat and well-pressed clothing was singing to himself, swinging and swaying as he stood. He was en route to visit his mother, he said. He seemed happy.

The train stopped at a station and police got on and began to pull the man off the train. He resisted, clearly frightened.

The police said there'd been a complaint of a disturbance. The man began to panic.

I spoke up, loudly, "He did nothing wrong!"

The police kept trying to get him out the door. The man began to recite his mother's phone number to another passenger, begging her to call, because his mother would be worried if he didn't show up.

I stood and took one step toward the police and the man, repeating myself, "He did nothing wrong!"

Others began to repeat that phrase, or things like it.

Others stood, too. Everyone was clearly upset, and not at the man, but at the police.

Several of us were clearly ready to follow them off onto the platform. No way were we leaving that man on his own.

What happened?

The police read the room. They released the man. The doors closed. We went on our way, all of us shaken. We tried to comfort the man.

The train went on to the next station. The man would get to see his mother after all.

JORDAN NEELY WON'T SEE anyone again.

Jordan Neely—a NYC street entertainer—was, by several accounts, in a mental health crisis on a subway car when he was choked to death by one white man while being restrained by two others.

No one spoke up for Jordan Neely, until around two and a half minutes into the chokehold, a Black man stepped back onto the train and calmly explained to the three white men that the chokehold was killing the man on the ground.

By the time they listened, Neely was already dead.

IT CAN BE hard to know what to do when adrenaline is pumping and a situation seems confusing.

It can be hard to speak up when our current overculture has taught us to outsource our responsibilities to each other to some shadowy "authority," whether that authority comes in the form of police, or immigration, or politicians...or three white men who have taken over a situation, causing harm.

But sometimes? We have to claim our own authority. We need to take a breath, find our courage, and speak. Loudly.

When we speak, that gives others the courage to speak up, too.

If one person had loudly insisted early on that Neely not be choked? Others may have joined them, and Neely might still be alive today.

I don't know this, of course. I was not there.

But I do know that we must try to do better by each other.

NEW YORK CITY knows what a chokehold did to Eric Garner. Florida knows what vigilantism looked like for Trayvon Martin.

Everyone in the US knows how violent some of our family members and neighbors are. There's a new story now, every day.

But what we don't hear or see enough are the stories where crisis was averted because someone spoke up, and others joined them.

I'd like more of those stories.

I ALSO WONDER what would have happened if a few people had tried to talk de-escalate the crisis. To talk to Neely. To ask him if he needed assistance.

I wonder what would have happened if someone had offered him food. Or asked him to sit down and talk.

That's hard, and I get it. I have a fair amount of on-the-ground experience with talking to highly agitated people in crisis. Most folks do not. It can feel scary to try to look beyond the surface behavior and re-humanize someone who is acting in erratic, perhaps frightening ways.

But if we are able to practice this? We can help others practice, too. Because if we're going to be vigilantes, let's be the kind who try to de-escalate a situation, instead of choking a man to death.

WE HAVE the power to help each other. We just have to choose it.

We have to practice when we are not in a crisis situation.

This starts in small ways: We talk to our neighbors. We ask someone on the street if they need help. We share what we have. We stop outsourcing our authority every time we encounter something annoying or upsetting.

We work to unlearn our racism, or our transphobia, or misogyny. We work to unlearn bigotry and fear.

We ask ourselves: "What would I do in a confusing situation where I feel that something's wrong?"

And then: We practice breathing. We practice speaking up. We practice asking others for help.

It doesn't always work. I've sometimes gone to people's aid with no backup. But oftentimes, other people join in. And we act as community.

And together, we save this world some pain.

May, 2023

PART 3

WHO BENEFITS?

THIRTEEN
CUI BONO?

There are children in the rubble. There are always children in the rubble.

There are bodies in the water. There are always bodies in the water.

There are families fleeing, sleeping in the cold, looking for safety, food, and home. There are always families fleeing.

There are multiple genocides happening as I type this, as the glaciers melt, the oceans rise, and the forests burn. There are piles of garbage choking land and sea. There are people working for pennies, barely able to survive. There are people living on street corners, and children going hungry, every day.

WHO BENEFITS FROM VIOLENCE, oppression, subjugation, genocide, pollution, and war? It is never the families, the workers, the ordinary people, or the children. It is multi national corporations, billionaires, weapons manufacturers, and exploiters of cheap labor. It is authoritarians and fascists who benefit from pain.

Every time we celebrate a billionaire, we tell the majority poor, "Your lives are forfeit to the machines of commerce. Your dreams and hopes don't matter. You belong to us now. Fall in line."

IN THE 1940S, the US government turned away Jews fleeing the Shoah, sending boats back onto the water. The US government now supports a genocidal political regime in Israel, not because Jewish people need a home, but because it is financially and strategically convenient.

In the 1990s and early 2000s, the US government lied about weapons of mass destruction, resulting in mass death in Iran, Iraq, and Afghanistan, and increased surveillance and control of its own citizens, the militarization and engorged funding of its police, and larger contracts for the machinery of war. The US went on to target and harass potential immigrants from the Middle East who tried to flee these created conflicts.

The US supports the current genocide in Darfur not because it cares, one way or another, about the people or causes there, but because the Saudi family funding the war has access the US wants, access to money and oil. The African continent, formerly a ground used to enslave free people for the sake of commerce, is rich in resources to be extracted. The people? The animals and plants? The climate? They don't much matter.

What matters are mineral rights, access, cheap labor, and oil.

Kleptocracy demands its tribute in blood and tears.

WHO BENEFITS FROM VIOLENCE, subjugation, and oppression?

Who benefits from dividing us from one another? Who benefits from building prisons and border walls?

Who benefits from news cycles, obfuscation, terror, and lies?

When we turn on our neighbors in anger, we must ask ourselves, "Who benefits?"

When synagogues or mosques are attacked, we must ask ourselves, "Who benefits?"

When we complain about protestors blocking bridges, we must ask ourselves, "Who benefits?"

When we sneer at immigrants, we must ask ourselves, "Who benefits?"

When we buy an eight-dollar shirt, we must ask ourselves, "Who benefits?"

When a Black man is shot down in the streets, we must ask ourselves, "Who benefits?"

When an Indigenous woman goes missing, we must ask ourselves, "Who benefits?"

When LGBTQIA rights are legislated out of existence, we must ask ourselves, "Who benefits?"

When prenatal care and abortion rights are curtailed, we must ask ourselves, "Who benefits?"

When language and culture are eradicated, and history gets rewritten in order to teach lies, we must ask ourselves, "Who benefits?"

When we see the images of slaughter, or drought, or burning, or drowning, or when children are taken from their families and passed on to the white and wealthy, we must ask ourselves, "Who benefits?"

It isn't most of us. It is never most of us. These actions benefit the very few, who leave the rest of us to suffer the consequences.

Oh, we may acquire temporary benefits by proxy—especially the more privileged among our ranks—but that is only to placate us, to keep us quiet, to hold the guillotines at bay.

GLOBAL SOLIDARITY REQUIRES us to remember that we are not the enemies of one another. No immigrant is coming to steal our jobs. No child is hiding a bomb in a school satchel. No doctor has a weapon's cache beneath the operating table.

Together, we can build a world where do not always need to live in fear. Where trauma does not define our every thought and action. Where teachers are valued, and people are housed.

Even in grief and anger, our faces are beautiful. I feel so many hearts, breaking. I see so many actions filled with hope: feeding people, protesting injustice, caring for a world in need.

Compassion and strength will lead us all toward justice, over time. I must believe this, because to do otherwise is to give over to despair.

Together, we are all we have.

November, 2023

FOURTEEN
LES MISÉRABLES
ON COLLECTIVE IMAGINATION AND ACTION

"We can overcome the structures that oppress us, but only if we are prepared to work hard to do so. We have the strength, we have the numbers and with the courage of our own convictions, we can regain the right to live our own lives."

— Crass, from *A Series of Shock Slogans and Mindless Token Tantrums*

I AM HEARTBROKEN. I am heartbroken, but not giving up.

My partner and I were at the grocery store this week. I was bagging our groceries when I saw motion and heard a "Whoa!"

Turning, I saw groceries scattered on the sidewalk just outside, one person standing, and another on the ground. I moved to rush outside and see if I could help, thinking someone had fallen. But then several store employees rushed outside, and it all became clear: someone had run out of the store with some food in their arms, chased by an employee who then got shoved to the sidewalk in a panic.

I think the person with the groceries got away, but was not sure.

As my partner and I walked out, I remarked, "Here we are. Les Misérables. No social safety net. People needing to steal food."

I felt angry, disgusted, and, by the time we got to our car, filled with heartbreak.

The life I live is fairly privileged, even though it should be ordinary. Sure, my household keeps track of the grocery bill, making sure we spend under a certain amount each month. We "shop the freezer," but we also don't have to carefully check prices. We are not the desperate parent who can't afford the locked-up formula or diapers. We aren't the person who ran out of the store today, arms cradling a few items of stolen food.

"EVERYONE HAS *the right to a standard of living adequate for the health and well-being of himself and of his family, including food, clothing, housing and medical care and necessary social services, and the right to security in the event of unemployment, sickness, disability, widowhood, old age or other lack of livelihood in circumstances beyond his control.*"

— from a Universal Declaration of Human Rights, article 25

IN THE CITY where I live—along with too many other US cities—public camping was just outlawed. Though, as the city already made regular sweeps of camps, trashing the only belongings people have to survive on a regular basis, I'm not certain what exactly is supposed to change. Except the already impoverished will get taken to jail and issued a fine.

These sweeps are so often timed before the most brutal weather changes, I have to wonder if it is not by design.

As I write this, Portland, Oregon, is in the midst of a record-setting heatwave. People I know are desperately trying to get cooling supplies to people on the streets and hotel rooms for as many as they can. People I know are redistributing air conditioners to elders and folks with disabilities who live in homes not designed for extreme temperatures.

Meanwhile, our city gave a massive, lucrative contract to an organization notorious for abuse in order to run city-approved encampments.

Every year, people die from extreme heat or cold, while a small percentage of us do our best to offer direct aid. We drop off food to the queer-safe warming shelter. We collect clean water for Wasco and Paiute elders, and send money to the collectives that are active on the streets, helping unhoused neighbors. We redistribute necessary goods to those who need them: old AC units, air purifiers for the smoky times, and heaters during winter's cold. We share refurbished computers and phones. We buy tablets for and gift books to children living in RVs....

There is an acknowledgement among us that we are all we have, so we'd better damn well show up.

"...WE *have become increasingly convinced that the most widespread, long-lasting, and fierce struggles are animated by strong relationships of love, care, and trust. These values are not fixed duties that can be imitated, nor do they come out of thin air. They arise from struggles through which people become powerful together.*"

— Nick Montgomery and Carla Bergman, from *Joyful Militancy: Building Thriving Resistance in Toxic Times*

I THINK the dream of government is that it is collective action. Government is supposed to take the ideas, interests, and resources from those who live within its arbitrary boundaries, and take care of those same people and the environment they live in.

It's a great thought that seems more efficient than a bunch of people getting together, ad hoc, to keep roads and sewer systems running, bridges safe, and to provide clean water, education, and shelter.

But repeatedly, we are thrown back—or I am, at any rate—on the realization that if we don't help each other, no one will. Bridges fail. Roads crumble. Tap water becomes undrinkable, and clean water is sold for pennies to bloated corporations that turn around and sell it back to those who should have free access to this life-giving liquid.

There is no savior. There is no one with all the answers. But there is us. There is collective action and mutual aid.

Is collective action sometimes a pain? Does it require time, energy, effort, thought, and commitment? Yes. It can. But collective action can also bring about fierce joy and a deep sense of satisfaction. There is joy in finding we can actually be of service to each other. We can share skills, thoughts, and resources. We can build systems of support.

I've seen disabled people organize refrigerator space and rides out of town when wildfire smoke chokes the sky. I've seen a group of schoolkids, smiling at a new-to-them computer that they didn't have before. I've seen youth organize against racism and to help their trans and queer friends. I've seen people checking on elders and doing grocery runs. I've seen free pantries filled with food. I've seen protest encampments sharing meals and medical care with unhoused neighbors....

There are so many wonderful things that I have seen. I'm sure we all have, if we are paying attention to the world around us.

"I BELIEVE *that all organizing is science fiction—that we are shaping the future we long for and have not yet experienced."*

— Adrienne Marie Brown, from *Pleasure Activism: The Politics of Feeling Good*

ALL OF MY personal long-term visions for a world that is and could be require collective imagination and collective action. These visions can be hard to hold on to because our social ills are legion and too many people buy into the systems of authoritarianism, punishment, and greed. Too many others are beaten down, simply trying to survive. Others are comfortable and don't want to look too closely at the problems they would rather went away.

They can never tell me where this elusive "away" might be.

So, I get angry. My friends get angry. We feel heartbroken and sometimes defeated.

It is right to feel grief and anger—necessary, even—but if we care for one another, we don't have the luxury of wallowing in it, not for long.

When grief and anger are rooted in love, they spur us into action. That's a very good thing.

I don't want to uphold a society where someone—like Victor Hugo's character, Jean Valjean—goes to prison for stealing a loaf of bread. I don't want to uphold a society where someone loses all their worldly goods and is slapped with a fine because they have no money and nowhere safe to sleep.

Together, we can build a different society. To defeat the forces of complacency and oppression, we must each do what we can. Our actions are more effective in the long term if we learn to work collectively, however small the action. All it takes is for a few friends and neighbors to make a choice to band together in mutual aid.

"MNÍ WIČÓNI. WATER IS LIFE."

— from the Lakota people

AS I WORKED on this essay on one of those scorching days, I noticed a parent with two young children—one in a stroller—sit down on the low containment wall outside our collective home, taking a moment to rest in the shade.

It was not yet the hottest part of the day, but it was still plenty hot. I knew there were cold drinks in the refrigerator. Carrying them out, I offered some cans to the little family. They accepted, with thanks.

Then I refilled a water dish for the birds and animals and went back inside.

It was one small act of kindness, and not nearly

enough to solve society's problems. But a cold drink on a hot day is still something. And some days, something is what we've got.

Portland, OR
July, 2024

FIFTEEN

WHO BENEFITS?

ON ART AND COMMERCE

Politics (from Greek: Πολιτικά*, politiká, 'affairs of the cities') is the set of activities that are associated with making decisions in groups, or other forms of power relations between individuals, such as the distribution of resources or status.*

If you think what you do for work, or the fact that you are out of work—or hustling, or making six or seven figures—isn't political... Or that the art and entertainment you enjoy doesn't promulgate human politics on every level...

You are deluding yourself.

In everything we do and don't do, we are relating to the cosmos, to the environment, and to people. We are engaging in relationships.

WHEN I WAS a young anarchist punk with a blue, curly, flat top and different patterns shaved on the sides monthly, I took my gold Dr. Marten's down to the Pacific Stock Options Exchange and got a job as a runner.

I really needed the money, and figured I could get a paid education about the US economic system.

The Options Exchange itself is a long story. I battled a lot there—including misogyny and homophobia—as you might imagine. Those stories must keep for another day.

Here are three small vignettes germaine to the conversation:

One: This was the late 1980s. The time of AIDS and apartheid South Africa.

In the screaming pits of the trading floor, beneath fluorescent lights and glowing green banks of computer screens, the market makers traded options. Not stocks. Not commodities. Not corn or steel or video games. Nothing rooted in anything tangible. They traded the option to maybe buy or sell the stock at a set price at a later date. The traders placed bets on whether a stock would go up or down by purchasing "calls" or "puts."

What were the traders called? Market Makers. They made the markets and affected the economy by sheer speculation.

I worked there for four years, in the end, running my own tiny business as an assistant to two market makers.

One day, I said to one of them, "How can you trade options on that Dutch Afrikaaner company?" He stood tall, puffed out his chest, and proudly proclaimed, "Commerce should be free of politics."

I looked at him, aghast. As if there was any such thing. As if the nation state and capitalism had not grown strong together, on the backs of enslaved people and through colonial, imperialist exploitation.

Story two: One day, the floor was going bonkers as usual. Yelling. Screaming. Heavy trading. One of my market makers was in the middle of a pit, trading frantically. He motioned. I waded into the seething, churning, screaming mass of white men. He handed me a ticket, and shouted in my ear for me to go buy Krugerrands. South African currency. Apparently the gold markets were volatile and he wanted in.

I paused. Time slowed. The screaming went on around me.

Inhaling, I looked him in the eyes and said, "No."

"What?"

"No."

His mouth pursed. His face went from red to purple. He threw down his stack of tickets, shoved past me, and stalked from the crowded pit to place the order himself.

Word spread around the trading floor like a California grass fire.

At the end of the day, when most everyone had left, and things grew quiet, the one Black trader on the floor walked up to me and shook my hand.

Read that last sentence again. The important part is "the one Black trader on the floor." One.

"Thank you," he said.

Three: The big crash of 1987 happened. I saw market makers who had bought new boats and Pacific Heights mansions—which I called "single family dwellings"—all of a sudden struggling, flailing, panicking. They were underwater. Drowning in debt.

They were also privileged as fuck, and would come out of it all okay. Eventually.

But in those panicked days, I just shook my head and typed the day's tickets into a late-80s computer as quickly as I could.

I was raised working poor. I'd been working myself since age 13. I knew how to stretch a loaf of bread. Though I was making more money than I ever had before, it was still a pittance compared to what the traders had just lost. I made just enough to afford a tiny studio apartment at the back of a garage, make motorcycle payments, and hang out in cafes after work, writing in endless notebooks.

Eventually, I was offered sponsorship to become a market maker.

Unwilling to sell my soul, I quit instead. I'd learned what I came for.

The lesson I learned?

The US economy is based on exploitation and gambling.

Having been raised by a parent with alcohol and gambling addictions, I'd had enough, and got a job in a natural foods warehouse, and later, a women-run peep show. And after that?

A soup kitchen, where I worked in exchange for room and board.

All of those jobs were entwined with the economics of human politics.

So is what I do now, writing books.

There is simply no way around it.

Commerce is never free of human politics. No matter

what it is, we have to ask:

Who has access?

Who benefits?

And who labors the most?

ARTISTS, filmmakers, sports figures, actors, and authors are always being told to shut up about politics. As if they can.

As if art is not all about human relationships, and as if human relationships are not political. We are the polis. There's no escaping it.

Every time I read a book, I notice how the author treats people in the police and military. Every time I watch a film, I notice what happens to the non-white characters, and if there even are any non-white characters. Or poor characters. Or trans characters. Every song tells a story about humans. Every painting and sculpture points to access, and available materials, and subject matter.

Jean-François Millet's painting, *The Gleaners*, is about the poorest of the poor, allowed to glean the fields for useable grain after the harvest. It would be the only grain their families had to eat. Wikipedia says: Millet unveiled *The Gleaners* at the Salon in 1857. It immediately drew negative criticism from the middle and upper classes, who viewed the topic with suspicion: one art critic, speaking for other Parisians, perceived in it an alarming intimation of "the scaffolds of 1793." The French Revolution ended in 1848, so for Millet to side with the working classes—when he depended upon the rich for his income—in 1857 was no small thing.

But of course, Millet was raised on a farm, and grew up farming. He knew where his sympathies lay.

Dickens. Shakespeare. Austen. All politics. Morrison. Walker. Rowling. Franzen. Stan Lee and Alison Bechdel. Whether you love or loathe them? All politics. Theaster Gates and Jasper Johns. Basquiat and Warhol. Gentillesci and Carrington. Public Enemy and Led Zeppelin. Clifton and Ginsberg and Shange and Wong. Sue Grafton and Walter Mosley. All politics.

What is taught? Who has access? All politics.

Not political? All politics.

I was privileged to watch the Alvin Ailey Dance Theater perform a dance about the killing of Black people by police. It was beautiful. Necessary. Art.

But any dance done on a stage in a theater is political. If you don't think so, study the history of European classical dance.

In his talk "Hip Hop, or Shakespeare?" the brilliant Akala reminds us that Shakespeare wrote for the working people, and spoke as the working people spoke. Who owns Shakespeare now? Well, he's considered posh, isn't he?

Again: who has access?

Rai music—which has its roots in working class folk music—flourished despite attempts to ban it. Songs about going to parties, dancing, and having a good time were considered dangerous. Political. A threat to the powers that be.

Poor, working people should be miserable, it seems.

Every bus stop ad. Every song. Every building in every neighborhood—and pay close attention, which urban neighborhoods have trees? Every video game. Every app. Every book.

It's all political. You just may have not noticed it before.

Art and politics that uphold the status quo we're used to? We like to say they are "just the world we live in" or "just the way things are."

But it has been designed, hasn't it?

We need to ask more often, of everything we encounter that is human made: who designed it? And who benefits?

And who pays the highest price?

June, 2021

SIXTEEN

THE SNOW CONTINUES TO FALL

The snow is one foot deep.
It graces the branches of trees.
It is beautiful and cold.

Some people sleep in tents, round hummocks topped with snow, some under one wool blanket. They don't feel safe in the emergency shelters.

Over the years, I've known other houseless people who don't feel safe in shelters. Braving cold, darkness, rain, and snow is often preferable to sleeping cheek-by-jowl with other humans who may do them violence.

And yet, they are houseless, on the street in the first place because our culture as a whole has done violence toward them. We have not made room for care, preferring money over inclusion, and punishment over community.

I SHOVELED my walk this morning, and my neighbor's too, because he's been ill with a high fever. Tomorrow, I may shovel the walk of the old man down the street if he still needs it. I can't make it downtown to offer more warmth to the street sleepers, but I can shovel walks for those unable to.

After shoveling for an hour, I leaned the broom and orange-handled shovel against the porch railing.

And there was the sparrow, seal-brown feathers puffed out and soft, lying dead on the blue planks. Did it seek shelter from the snow on our porch and die from the cold?

A WOMAN DIED from exposure in this city last week. She was found naked in a parking garage downtown. It is said that one of the stages of hypothermia is the feeling that you are burning up inside.

People undergoing hypothermia often remove their clothing, trying to get relief. When the body reaches this state of heat loss, the heart often simply stops beating.

The woman's name was Karen Lee Batts; she struggled with mental illness and was evicted from her apartment in a disabled housing complex for owing $338 in back rent.

She's one of four who've died outside since the cold arrived in Oregon this month.

WHENEVER WE HEAR someone say that the poor don't work hard enough, or that charity is justice, that shelters and soup kitchens are good enough, that basic income, health care, education, and housing are not rights, but privileges for those savvy enough to work the systems of empire...I want us to pause, and ask if in our hearts, we feel these statements to be true.

And I want us to recall Karen Lee Batts, who died alone at age 52 for the lack of 338 dollars.

I want us to recall Maria Fernandes, dead from carbon monoxide poisoning, who was only trying to get a little rest by napping in her car between the three jobs she worked in order to survive.

Then I want us to recall the gold-plated bathrooms. The thousand-dollar dinners. The billions stolen. Millions exploited. And I want us to ask why the ultra-wealthy deserve more than Karen or Maria.

My answer is: They don't.

My answer is: We need to restructure our values.

My answer is: There should be neither the extremely wealthy nor the impoverished. There is no reasonable excuse for either.

My answer is: Let's break this fucking system and build the world anew.

Let's build a kinder, more just, more compassionate place, where there are homes, and food, and schools, and care for all.

MEANWHILE, I write this on a sleek machine made by people exploited and overworked half the world away. I listen to music on a device that uses material hand mined by children and decimates the habitats of mountain gorillas.

Meanwhile, I have a warm home to return to tonight.

OUTSIDE, the snow continues to fall.

It is quite beautiful.

Portland, OR
January, 2017

SEVENTEEN
ON PROPERTY AND PROTEST

Disclosure: property destruction is not a tactic I personally use, so that colors what I'm about to say. Take or leave my opinion as you will.

I WANT to talk about property destruction.

The first thing that needs to be said:

In looking at property destruction, we must always first look at the major destroyers of communities, land, water, and sky. Monsanto. Wells Fargo. The US Federal government. White Supremacy. The police. Imperialism. Plutocracy... We can add to this list for days. Any critique of, or support for, property destruction must be grounded in the awareness of who the most destructive culprits actually are.

They are not masked people in the streets.

Second, I want to distinguish between property destruction as spontaneous uprising—an emotional response to direct brutal oppression and disenfranchisement—and planned action. A few instances of spontaneous uprising are the rebellions in Watts, Ferguson, or at Stonewall. These are all examples of people with little recourse, who've been pushed too far, for too long, and finally snap. "A riot is the language of the unheard," as Dr. King said.

Now I want to speak of property damage as a form of planned protest:

My support for and critique of property damage both come from asking the same questions: "Is it strategic action?" and "What is the aim?"

One example of effective and strategic property damage comes from French radical farmer José Bové. He's done many strategic actions of destruction. My favorite is when he gathered a group to dismantle a McDonalds being built in their village. The McDonalds threatened their small village industries and their commerce, and also signified the encroachment of global capitalism that was a threat to their way of life.

This sort of strategic property destruction is a very effective tactic, with a clear aim.

For me, smashing windows of small, upscale businesses once a year is not good strategic action. Does it drive out gentrifiers and displacers? It doesn't seem to. In most cases, they sweep up, collect insurance money, and move on.

Smashing smaller local businesses also serves to alienate the community, pushing them further from solidarity and action. For example, I've heard directly from Black community members upset that a local clothing design shop and store—that was Black owned and contributed to various community projects—was targeted during protests because it was seen by white activists as part of Black neighborhood gentrification. The action pushed community members away from any possible engagement or solidarity.

Targeting large banks or major corporations on a regular basis as part of an ongoing series of actions? I would feel differently about that, and many community members might also feel differently, especially if there was an educational arm releasing propaganda to explain that this large bank chain was targeted because of predatory lending or foreclosures.

A side question that crops up in this discussion is: "Am I directly putting others in danger right now?"

Here's one example of what I mean by the second question: people who stand way behind a crowd and throw projectiles at police from relative safety while putting folks in the front in direct danger. I'm not okay with that at all. That is reckless cowardice.

A second example happens often when white activists refuse to take leadership from or pay attention to more marginalized groups. At post-election 2016 actions in Oakland, militant African leadership encouraged white activists to not engage in property damage. They called for "revolutionary discipline" for a variety of reasons. Things were still smashed. That happens. Often.

The next day, when members of the African-led group went to set up for another action, they were targeted by police, threatened, and almost had their sound equipment impounded and truck towed.

So another thing to keep in mind, besides "is it

strategic and what is our aim?" is this: Who might we be putting at risk? Are there people of color in the group, or in leadership? Are trans people present? People with disabilities? Undocumented immigrants? Children?

If the answer to any of those is "yes," it is best to not use a large action as cover and protection for property destruction. There are other times to do strategic action if that is your choice of tactic.

We can't let the wish to destroy undermine efforts to build solidarity. Being run by high emotion or inflated ego is not strategic or effective action.

In summation:

While I don't engage in property destruction myself, over many years I've been friends with those who do (Catholic Plowshares activists, I'm looking at you). These were always in critique of the larger destructive systems. To not engage that larger critique is to miss the point entirely, and only pits us against one another and plays directly into the hands of those who most directly oppress our comrades and the most vulnerable members of our interlocking communities.

I would like to see people working toward solid aims. On occasion, it feels like some people are just acting out. Also, not having strategic aim makes it much easier for infiltrators/agitators/provocateurs to enter our ranks and incite people to non-strategic action or putting others in danger.

In my opinion, if we are going to build long-term, sustainable, society-changing activist communities, we must also always ask, "What purpose/whom does this action serve?" And, "What is our plan?"

I hope that anyone engaging in, critiquing, or supporting planned property destruction considers these sorts of questions.

In solidarity. Toward love, equity, and justice.

Oakland, CA
November, 2016

EIGHTEEN

TEAR IT DOWN

ASSAULT, VIOLENCE, & HEALING IN EMPIRE

It's been a rough and traumatic few weeks, following a rough and traumatic year, following a rough and traumatic several decades, or hundreds of years.

It all depends upon your perspective.

YOU THINK it can be fixed. Amended. Reformed.

It can't.

RAPE. Harassment. Assault. Murder. Degradation. Trauma. Shame.

THERE IS nothing about our current systems that is not working exactly the way it is meant to.

These systems are meant to punish the poor.

These systems are meant to exploit women and female presenting people.

These systems are designed to shame non-alpha men and male presenting people.

These systems are designed to prey upon the weak and to reinforce their weakness at every turn.

These systems are designed to put psychopaths and abusers in positions where they have power over others.

These systems are designed to support constant predation, violence, and the reign of fear.

These systems are designed to kill.

WHEN A COUNTRY'S economy is largely set up to serve the military and the ultra-wealthy, how can we not expect that it would filter down into mass shootings, the murder of women and femmes, the constant killing of Black, brown, and Native citizens by police, the torture of children, the rape of janitors working the night shift, and the crushing of the working class?

Predators run this world. We praise and reward them for it. Every single system is set up to show predators how much we care. About them.

These systems will not change. These systems cannot and will not be reformed.

These systems must be toppled to the ground by the very people whom they have preyed upon. These systems must be broken by our refusal to go along. To cover up. To feel ashamed. To wish that we were wealthy and powerful and gleaming with the sleekness only brought about by living off the suffering of others.

"KEVIN SPACEY and his brother were abused," they said.

I have no doubt that this is true. And you know what else? I've also been abused. So have too many of my friends to begin counting, and we do our utmost best to not abuse others.

"Dylann Roof will get the death penalty," it has been reported. He killed, so he should be killed?

I will never trust the state to do anything other than kill, and I will never trust that the state will mete out anything approaching justice.

"We demand justice," others have said.

But what does justice look like within these systems? Does prison offer justice? Does economic ruin offer justice? Does public humiliation offer justice? Does death offer justice?

No. All these things offer is revenge, and revenge is not enough. Revenge does not bring balance. Revenge does not restore harmony. Revenge does not offer healing.

Revenge is empty, promising much, and delivering almost nothing.

We currently have no justice systems in place.

We have no systems that offer healing.

We have no systems that actually keep communities healthy, safe, and thriving.

All we have are ashes, flecked with gold.

WE BARELY EVEN HAVE SYSTEMS OF accountability, let alone, justice.

The sickness we live with is so endemic and deeply rooted, it can be difficult to find a different way. It is difficult to even think on it, let alone imagine it.

But that different way already exists.

It is called Sankofa.

It is called Ho'o pono-pono.

It is called Tikkun Olam.

It is called Restorative Justice. Healing. Repair.

We see people banding together, enacting these restorative methods. These people try to feed one another, and help one another heal, and cultivate joy – all in the midst of the crushing systems that make all of these processes as difficult as possible.

And then we are surprised and saddened when these efforts "fail."

But they do not fail. They are crushed. Temporarily.

Because people always find a way to love again.

The dandelion will always find a way to crack the concrete smothering its roots.

THE POLICE CANNOT BE REFORMED.

Prisons cannot be reformed.

The military will not keep us safe.

These systems offer only more abuse, harm, and degradation.

Prisons, courts, and policing will never offer justice.

Big business? The rewarding of predators?

That cannot be reformed, or fixed. The blows cannot be softened.

SO WHAT DO WE DO?

We start over. We free all but the most violent prisoners (we'll deal with them later, once we have better systems in place). We offer a safety net. We offer housing, education, health care, and a basic income. We offer mental health resources. We offer a chance to heal and make amends.

We set up systems of restorative justice, where people are trained to not simply resolve conflicts, but heal the damages that conflict has caused.

We train ourselves toward different ways of power.

We train ourselves to value things other than money and fame.

We insist that caring for one another is important.

We muster our will and look to indigenous leadership and Black wisdom, and to other sources that offer real solutions.

We say, "We've fucked up, badly. This whole society is a fucking mess." And then we make what amends we can, and white and/or middle and/or upper-class people shut up and *do* what the poor, and the indigenous, and Black, and trans, and disabled people have been shouting at us to do for hundreds of years:

We build a society based on health and well-being

instead of punishment and greed. We build a society based on restoration of harmony. We remember what it feels like to be whole.

We abolish – firmly – all of the systems that only serve to oppress and terrorize the most vulnerable among us.

We begin the very real work planning the society we want to build. Not as a utopia. Not as pie-in-the-sky. As the reality we aim to live in.

Prisons and courts and bombs and drones and the stockpiling money built on slave labor will not save us. Only love will.

EMPIRE IS ALREADY CRUMBLING under its own weight.

You think it can be fixed. Amended. Reformed.

It can't. Tear it down. Now is our chance.

Then, if we have the collective will...we can build something new.

November, 2017

NINETEEN
THEY HAVE BEEN TURNED TO SWANS

And their bodies, slowly, painfully, shifted then from fingers and elbows, and biceps, turning into wings. Their feet were webbed. Their necks grew long with weeping.

They were become as refugees. Beings seeking refuge from whatever storms battled their countries, their families, their hearts. They were refugees because of greed and fear and the wars held in the hearts of women and men.

And off they flew.

The land was dry. So dry. There was no food. Their houses were riddled with bullet holes and danger.

They walked many kilometers. They swam. They ran. They hid. They froze and burned. Their feet became so twisted with blisters and hard use that sometimes, some days, they wished that they had wings.

And their weapons were thrown into deep pools. As offerings for whatever Gods might care. As prayers that peace would come into their land.

But the land that they called home was burning. Crumbling. Disintegrating from its grief.

They flew across the sea. There was no place for them to land. No family but the wings that beat beside them.

The only homes they had were in the hands that gripped their own, pulling them across scorched earth. The only homes they had were in the arms that held them as they crossed choppy, gray-green waters, searching hopelessly for land.

The Children of Lir flew on, stopping only to rest upon the waves of the great sea.

While in Ireland, our first pilgrimage stop in Dublin was to the Garden of Remembrance, dedicated to "all who gave their lives for Irish Freedom." A long pool holds mosaics of swords, spears, and shields thrown into the water. And at the end is a huge statue of the Children of Lir, shifting from human child bodies into swans taking flight.

That statue, a statue of forced exile, is a stunning reminder of the cost of freedom. For the Irish, as for many people around the globe, part of the cost of freedom is not just death, it is the inability to return home.

Standing on those grounds, with the faces of Syrian refugees in my mind, I couldn't get over the pain and power of it all.

"There are 60 million refugees in the world right now," one of our circle said. We paused in our circle, and breathed that in.

Their voices carried the timbre of the cries of swans. The songs they sang were human. Their father was bereft.

Each day on our pilgrimage, we read a poem. We sat in

pubs come evening and listened and sang songs. Too many Irish songs and poems carry this sense of the loss of life and home. Every Irish song and poem carries a sense of longing.

Footsore and weeping, we call these forced exiles something other than human. We call them refugees, migrants, victims, émigrés, immigrants, aliens, illegals, cowards. Yet, within their swan bodies live a humanity as large and small as ours. Hopes. Dreams. Fears. Ambition. The need for shelter for their children, and a place to work in safety. They are humans just like us. It is our own fear and greed that call them something other.

We want to think it was not greed or fear that cast them out and set them on their way, and yet, it is. We want to think we have nothing to do with their plight. And yet, we do.

Their hearts shifted inside their feathered breasts, from human hearts to hearts best suited for the flight of swans.

Climate change and war. Outsourcing of jobs, and chaining children to factory machines. Burnt lands and bombs. We cause it all, whether by active force, by silence, or complicity. Mostly, we cause it by the simple living of our lives in these towns and homes with our cars and refrigerators and air conditioning, and heating, and fracking, and mining, and blasting.

We cause their exile with every light we turn on because we cannot face the darkness. Or because sometimes it is just nice to have the option of more light.

She feared her new husband would not love her anymore. That she would lose her place, her power. And so she turned them with her witchery.

Corporate masters and government leaders live in greed and fear. Sometimes overt and sometimes subtle, their actions ripple out across the land and into water. They fear a loss of home and love. They fear a fall from grace. So they fill the void with cries of more. More money. A greater sense of power. More resources. Hoarding everything until, for the wandering children, everything is gone.

By taking up the Druid's staff, she tapped their milky children's shoulders, and turned them into swans.

There is an image of a man clutching his children, weeping from his ordeal and from the relief of finally getting his family back to land.

"He should go back home," people have said, not thinking for one second that this planet is home to us all, and we have all had a hand in making large portions of it inhospitable for habitation.

And this displacement of human life is only going to get worse. It is only going to increase.

She exiled them for 900 years.

We have sent arms and bombs to chase people from their homes. We have ensured that drought scourges their land, so the farmers can grow no more food. We have ensured all of this even as in our own cities, people are being displaced, turned into migratory birds searching for places to work and to name home.

We are both the fearful stepmother who turned her husband's children into swans and we are the swans ourselves.

By the time they returned home, their home was long

destroyed. Rubble. Crumbling back to earth. They would never know their father's touch again.

I did a ritual with a group of pilgrims in the middle of the city that day. We held hands and prayed for all the migrants, the refugees, the expatriots, and immigrants. We sang for them, lengthening our necks and lifting our human faces to the gray Dublin sky. We let our voices rise.

Beside us, cast in bronze, the children's bodies turned into swans and stretched out toward the sky.

Dublin, Ireland
October, 2015

PART 4

ON WHITE SUPREMACY

TWENTY
AN OPEN LETTER TO WHITE AMERICA

I am sending out a call for compassion.

I am sending out a call for reason.

I am sending out a call for an expansion of our presence with one another.

I am sending out the remembrance of the threads of our connection. We are not isolated beings on this planet. Collectively, in our gorgeous variance, we make up this living organism we call life.

I barely slept last night. After marching in the streets of Oakland, I came home, checked in with loved ones, ate something, and tuned in to what was happening in Ferguson. And what continued happening in Oakland until the small hours, and what was happening in 160 other cities.

When writing about these topics before, I've remarked that my troubled sleeplessness has nothing on the pain and anguish felt by Black and brown parents, lovers, and friends.

This morning, a woman tweeted that she thought she

was okay, until she saw a group of children walking to school and burst into tears. I don't know what it is like to live inside that sort of fear, anguish, grief, and pain.

But it doesn't take much for me to imagine it.

When Rodney King was beaten and Los Angeles was on fire, I felt concern, but I felt that concern from a distance. I didn't have enough context for a deeper state of empathy. It took the shooting of unarmed Oscar Grant to begin to turn me around. It took rushing to a city council meeting to hear Jeralynn Blueford speak right after the killing of her son, Alan. It took marching in the streets of Sacramento and Oakland with multiple families of people killed by police. Whether the victims of police killings were men, women, straight, gay, cis, or trans, they had one thing in common: most of these beloved family members were Black. Some were brown. Very few were white. All of the families were in pain.

In the past few years, I've been forced, for the first time in my white, working-class (now middle-class), activist life, to actually confront the reality of life for Black and brown people in the United States. And I still don't live inside that reality and am not forced to deal with it daily. I am not a parent, frightened that a child might not make it home from the store. I am not a man who knows that just walking out the door might get me shot. I am not a woman—cis or trans—who knows that asking for help from police might just get me raped or killed.

You may not live within that reality either. It may be hard for you to even imagine it is real. But I'm asking you to make a stronger effort to gaze into that reality.

The extrajudicial killing of Black and brown people by police is not a sometime thing. It is said that every twenty-eight hours a Black person is killed by police or security agencies. Just looking at the news and at my Twitter feed, this is not so hard to believe. Are all cops bad people? No. Are all cops racist? No. But the system they work within is. This is the system that stops and frisks Black and brown men in large cities every single day. The system that incarcerates and disenfranchises Black men at horrifically high rates. The system that tells Black women their bodies are both loathed and admired, but are not their own to hold and keep.

Property.

Some people say, "get over slavery," and yet, Black people in the United States are still treated as less than human. They are repeatedly treated as commodities to make money from and to use.

The rallying cry of "Black Lives Matter" is important because, within these systems, they clearly don't. Black lives, in the United States, only matter to the systems of capitalism and imperialism as resources to be exploited and cast off.

Black. Lives. Matter.

Someone on my Facebook feed commented this week that all life is sacred, and we shouldn't preference Black people as being special. I replied that all life is indeed sacred, but some life is more in danger. Black people's lives are more in danger. This is simple reality. In this, I'm not appealing to empathy or emotion, I'm drawing upon facts. This is not something over which we can "agree to disagree." This is truth. I can offer multiple reports for every single statement I made a couple of paragraphs back.

Someone commented that they simply don't understand people burning their communities down.

To that, I need to comment here: if you cannot understand what it means to fear for your own life or the lives of your children and friends on a daily basis from your own government, that you pay for, who has authority over you when it should be in place to serve you, a government that treats you and your children and friends as less than human, and calls them "animals" and "demons" or "those people," then I guess I can comprehend why property damage bothers you. But I can't condone your thinking this. I will go so far as to say that you are wrong.

We have to see the systems. We have to at least try to see the lived experience that is so different from our own.

When the system has not only failed you, but has actively put your well-being and your life, and your families' lives, in danger, how exactly are you supposed to respond? By trusting in that system?

I don't find random property damage done from grief and anger to be helpful or useful as a political tactic. That said: human life is worth more than human property. Always. In the United States? Particularly in White America? We seem to have reversed their importance, placing property over humanity, at least when those humans have darker skin.

(Aside: I won't talk about the use of strategic property damage, as used by anti-war Catholic Plowshares activists or French farmers protesting the building of McDonald's in their towns. And I won't expand here on how rioters at pumpkin festivals, or after World Series games or hockey championships, are treated in an "aw shucks" manner by mainstream media and police. Looking up any of these should illustrate the difference between protests against state violence and "revelers" smashing windows and setting things on fire.)

Black and brown and Indigenous people are fighting for their lives.

Legal recourse has not worked. Asking nicely has not worked. Respectability politics has not worked. Waiting quietly has not worked. Being three times better or working twice as hard has not worked. The message is clear: your ancestors were brought here for our use, and we will never let you belong. This message, of course, comes from systems whose foundations were formed on the genocide of the First Nations peoples who are also, despite being the original human inhabitants on this continent, still oppressed and treated as if they do not belong.

White America has a problem, and that problem is ourselves.

Our myopia, our lack of empathy, our inability to see the ways in which we live in arrogance, is literally killing people in the streets.

Please. I entreat us all. Do your very, very best to understand this. Because we are failing miserably at the task of community. We are failing miserably at the task of building something fine. We are failing to be fully human.

I'm saying this even to those of us with Black or brown friends. I'm saying this even to those of us who try to educate ourselves about the horrors of the prison industrial complex or the effects of systemic racism. Even we need to actually imagine: what is it like to feel afraid to send my child to the store, knowing they might end up being killed by an agent of our government?

I'm not speaking of random violence. I'm not speaking of violence from or among people with fairly equal social power—that happens to every group. I'm speaking here of fear of violence from people who carry the badges of social authority and who back that up with guns, Tasers, clubs, tear gas, and armored vehicles in the midst of a system that believes, at its core, that you are less human than people with lighter skin.

I call upon compassion.

I call upon empathy.

I call upon reason.

I pray we remember this: we are all connected.

I pray that we remember: we are responsible for one another's well-being.

November 2014

TWENTY-ONE
WHITE SUPREMACY KILLED TAMIR RICE
(AND LET TWO COPS GO FREE)

"White Supremacy is an historically based, institutionally perpetuated system of exploitation and oppression of continents, nations, and peoples of color by white peoples and nations of the European continent, for the purpose of maintaining and defending a system of wealth, power, and privilege."

– Elizabeth Martinez

"When you are 12 years old? You are little, but you learn fast. Be off the street by five o'clock. Move fast if you are little and black. Because the police will get you..."

– Bill Russell (Go Up for Glory, 1966)

. . .

Samaria Rice is grieving. We should all be grieving with her. We should all be angry. We should all be filled with rage at a system that allows government employees to drive up and shoot a twelve-year-old boy and face no consequences. We should be filled with anger that a grand jury can look at such a case and decide that the actions of the police were justified.

Racism exists because we let it.

Hatred exists because we let it.

Despair exists when we run out of ways to cope.

Anger is a fuel that sets despair on fire.

I'm so angry. Angry at the racism in my own family and in my communities. Angry at the comfort I live in bought by complicity with systems of abuse and destruction. Angry at the brutalization and murder by police of men and women in my city. Angry at systems that give too much to too few and too little to too many. Angry that in a country as rich as mine, people still live on the streets in the cold. Angry that in a country as rich as mine, children go to school hungry. Angry that in a country as rich as mine, we can't find a way to share the wealth, but must hold people down, expensive shoes on their necks, until they submit.

Angry that, whether submitting or standing up for themselves, too many people end up dead. Dead at the hands of government employees whom we pay for this service of preying on those considered weaker or less worthy of love and protection.

Community organizer Tur-Ha Ak talks about primary predators and secondary predators. The primary predators are the main beneficiaries of white supremacy: politicians, police, oligarchs and plutocrats, multi-billionaires, and CEOs.

"The PRIMARY PREDATOR is White Power Structures & all agencies & institutions that have actively, knowingly & systematically disenfranchised our communities. Disenfranchisement is achieved through the frequent use of every form of violence & criminal behavior attributed to the alleged 'criminal' element and more.

Then there are SECONDARY PREDATORS, or those who have been created under systems of disenfranchisement. They engage life how they've been taught; through the experiences of oppression. The former prey, now turned predator, subjugates the community in order to survive, or to mimic the material successes of the primary predatory. When dealing with the SECONDARY PREDATOR, it is important to remember that they exist largely due to our lack of organizing power & capabilities."

I want to explain a little bit about white supremacy here:

The current working definition of racism is not simple bigotry or chauvinism, but rather bigotry + relative systemic power (seen in the prison industrial complex, stop and frisk, red-lining communities, white nepotism, etc.). When we speak of white supremacy, our conversation is not about men in white sheets, but about all of the systems that uphold whiteness as the ideal and the norm.

White supremacy is at play every time people complain that there are Black or brown characters messing up their books or movies. White supremacy is at play every time Black or brown people are treated as criminals by default. White supremacy says that the white experience—particularly the white male experience, but even such movements as white feminism—is universal and that other experiences are secondary and less important.

White supremacy is at play when officers can kill Black and brown people and not face consequences. It is even at play if the officers in question are *non-white.* Why? Because all officers belong to a white supremacist (and patriarchal) system, a system that favors wealthy white men above all others.

As philosopher bell hooks writes: "The term 'white supremacy' enables us to recognize not only that black people are socialized to embody the values and attitudes of white supremacy, but we can exercise 'white supremacist control' over other black people."

White supremacy means that the entire society does all it can to make sure that wealthy white men have good lives and that *the rest of us are supposed to aspire to lives that look just like those.*

This is to our detriment. White supremacy locks everyone into lives where our Black and brown friends and colleagues live in greater danger of being killed, raped, and harassed. Of having stress-related health problems that often lead to early death. Of being at greater risk for discrimination in housing, schooling, and employment.

All of this diminishes community. All of this makes us less whole. White supremacy also traps those of us who are not the ultra-wealthy minority in cycles of want and greed, causing us to value things that destroy humans, animals, and earth. White supremacy destroys whole cultures via economic and cultural imperialism, missionary activity, exploitation of human thought, culture, and labor, the erosion of the commons, and the insistence that white European countries deserve to consume the bulk of the earth's resources.

It may seem as though I'm ranging far afield from the topic of the unconscionable murder of Tamir Rice, but in order to comprehend the operation of white supremacy, we must examine its scope.

This isn't just about out of control police violence and brutality. We can't try to "solve police violence" because police violence is only one small and deadly symptom of the large and destructive force that is white supremacy.

Tamir Rice is dead because all of white America pulled the trigger. That includes me, because I benefit from the systems of white supremacy.

Timothy Loehmann, Frank Garmback, Timothy McGinty, and the police dispatchers are all agents of white supremacy. They are all part of the primary predatory system written of by Tur-Ha Ak.

As I wrote in my "Open Letter to White America" in November 2014:

When the system has not only failed you, but has

actively put your well-being and your life, and your families' lives in danger, how exactly are you supposed to respond? By trusting in that system?

I wrote those words about Black Americans, but really, none of us should trust this system anymore. The systems of white supremacy serve so very few of us in the long term. All of white supremacy's promises to us are lies, fairy tales told by the .001% who hoard wealth and economic power.

White supremacy is not a dream; it is a nightmare we must all awaken from.

If it weren't for white supremacy, Samaria Rice would be enjoying the company of her son right now, and Tajai Rice would not be living with the trauma of running to help her brother and being tackled, handcuffed, and locked in a police car while she watched Tamir die.

There is story after story of a white person with a gun who has lived—including white people who have shot at police and white people who have killed multiple other people—and been taken into police custody without being shot, let alone killed.

If it weren't for white supremacy, Alan Blueford, Sandra Bland, Aiyanna Jones, Kayla Moore, Eric Garner, Oscar Grant, Idriss Stelley, Yuvette Henderson, Andy Lopez, and thousands of others might still be alive. If it weren't for white supremacy, Fred Hampton would not have been assassinated. If it weren't for white supremacy, thirteen women might not have been sexually assaulted by Officer Daniel Holtzclaw. If it weren't for white supremacy, the Middle East might be a different place, and refugees might not have been created, let alone refused safe harbor.

"When a child dies, the living must not rest until they have purged the poison that dared harm such a one."

– Mumia Abu Jamal

SO WHAT DO WE DO? We purge the poison.

We begin by noticing white supremacy around us, and then inside of us. And we ask ourselves, "What can I do to change my relationship to white supremacy and how do I begin to squeeze the oxygen from it, taking away some of its strength?"

We must see how the Primary Predators that Ak speaks of operate. This is particularly important for white people who mainly live and work and read and listen to other white people. The bubble of whiteness can keep us from seeing and hearing the true messages of white supremacy, just like the fish fails to see the water it swims in.

In expanding our scope, we begin to awaken our senses to deeper truths, including the truths about how our non-white brothers, sisters, and siblings live and love under and within these systems of domination and terror.

In expanding our scope, we awaken to the fact that our values and norms are not the norms of everyone and every thing.

Our egos can be useful, resilient things. They help us create, and keep us strong. Our egos can also be weak and filled with fear or hubris, and with the sure knowledge that everything in the world centers around us. That viewpoint enables our fragile egos to cease to see the lives of others as having the same importance our lives do. We dehumanize. We steal. We hold power over. We seek only our own comfort.

We cease to have compassion. We become predators.

The antidotes to the poison of white supremacy lie in scrupulous self-examination, in raising our awareness of the systems at play, in admitting our part in these damaging systems, and listening to those most affected by the damaging systems.

And then: We invoke hope, imagination, and creativity to counter the systems of harm.

What kind of world do you want to live in? What values do you strive to uphold? It is time to ask yourself, every single day, which side am I on, and what am I doing to dismantle white supremacy within my own heart and mind, within my family, within my workplace, within my communities, and within my country?

Diminishing the power of white supremacy begins every time we buy our children books with diverse characters. It begins each time we offer kindness to a stranger. It begins each time we show up in opposition to brutality. It begins each time we listen to someone whose life experience is different from our own.

Priestess Katrina Messenger asks us, “What choices are we making in order to survive?”

What choices will we make today, to help keep a child alive? To keep a parent from grief?

What choices will we make to seek out truths outside our echo chambers and create change in our communities?

How will we do our best to keep every twelve-year-old's heart alive and beating with our own?

Our answers to these questions will play out over the next several decades. Act now to shift the narrative of the future.

December, 2015

TWENTY-TWO
A RACIST

"People act like racism is always something you choose to do

instead of a system that has indoctrinated you with unconscious behaviours."

– Chelsea Vowel (âpihtawikosisân)

I recently read a novel in which the author had a character say things like, "It wasn't darkest Africa!" and also used the term "white slavery." A few weeks later, I noticed this author on social media doing some support work for diversity in publishing. Incongruous? Yes. Unusual? No.

Musician Florence Welch has a song I like, "No Light, No Light." Several years ago, I wanted to share it, and the easiest way was via the video, which I finally watched. Instantly horrified at the wash of racism coming across my computer screen, I paused, thinking, *How did this get all the way from idea, through production, and to release with no one saying anything?*

Then I did a little research. Had Florence + the Machine apologized for the video? Not that I ever saw. All I found were a bunch of comments by fans saying, "Florence isn't a racist!" What I think the fans meant by that was "Florence isn't a bad person!"

Because, you see, to be "a racist" is to be a bad thing.

Someone works for a mission, or an NGO, or does "voluntourism." They have the best intentions. They want to do good in the world. They might actually do some things that are good. But in the midst of all that do-gooding, they set themselves apart from the very people for whom they claim to have compassion. They are treating them as lesser. As though the person visiting is Lady Bountiful come to save the poor natives. Daenerys Targaryen come to free the slaves. And as though they know what's best for people whose culture they barely know.

The systems themselves are racist, and influence everyone within them.

There is rarely the person or group who asks the locals what they want and need and what skills they have in their communities. The missionary, or NGO, or volunteer/tourist group often tromps right in and makes changes that can decimate the local economy. Even with the best intentions.

And then these (most often white) people leave, with lovely photos of themselves surrounded by the dark-skinned people whom they so kindly helped.

Is each of these individuals "a racist"?

Ah. You see, there is the problem. There are people who will tell you—if they trust you, or just don't care what you think—that they hate Mexicans, or Arabs, or people of African descent. But most people aren't like that. Most people will say that they either actively like, or at least, have no issue with non-white people. "I'm not a racist!" they declaim. "I have Black friends!"

Just like the author I mentioned, or like Florence + the Machine or the voluntourist or NGO worker would, I imagine.

Part of the trouble we have is that phrase, "a racist." Almost no white person thinks they are. Including me, despite my many racist fuckups over the years.

Just as almost no one thinks they are "a sexist," or "transphobic," or any number of words meant to convey the ways in which humans belittle, or degrade, or insult, or ignore or "Other" human beings who may be different than they are.

Yet we do this. All the time. We fail to see the lived experiences of others, fail to listen to their words. We just assume the template of our lives is the template everyone should live by.

We think we know what's best.

(And as an aside to this conversation: No one ever thinks they're "a rapist," either. Just ask most people who rape.)

The trouble is that when we think of "a racist," we think of a Klan member, or a white man with a Swastika tattooed on his forehead. And being "a racist" is a defining thing. It colors how we think of the whole of the person.

There are many reasons why I am not quick to call anyone "a racist" and mostly it's that it is a totalizing move. A noun, rather than a verb.

Do I think most of us are riddled with prejudices, biases, and bad cultural training? Yes. Do I think most people actively hate and fear and attack people who are not like them? Those people exist, for sure, but I don't think most of us are that way.

Most of us are not that extreme. We are people who engage in systems of racism, and our thoughts and behaviors are tinged with it. There is no way they can't be. We have racist attitudes. We have internalized bigotry, and cultivated tastes and fears, all of which end up affected by what folks rightly call white supremacy.

White people act in ways that are racist and oppressive, often without even thinking of it.

White supremacy is, once again, not just the white-hooded, cross-burning person we used to call a "white supremacist", a person who believes white people are rulers and other, more dark-skinned people are subhuman.

White supremacy stems from this: all the systems we live in are set up to give preference to whiteness, and to make it the standard.

White people are in more movies and books, as

multifaceted, living, breathing characters. When Black or brown characters show up in books and movies, they are often based on tropes. Similar things can be said for disabled people, or LGBTQ people, or often even heterosexual, cisgender white women.

Whiteness is the measure of beauty, of intellectual prowess, of success. Magazines tell us that light skin and thin noses are more beautiful. Silicon Valley tells us that white men's ideas are just naturally better. So do universities. So does the publishing industry. How many publishers have Black editors on staff? Almost none. I could go on and on with examples, if we had time.

I've written many essays about systemic racism, police brutality, and the impact of white supremacy. Many other people have written even better things. It's hard to not just repeat myself, because these basic concepts are the backbone for any conversation we have on race. But I want to point to something slightly different, and hope you'll take the time to do some research on your own.

I want to go back to what Metis writer Chelsea Vowel is speaking of: unconscious behaviors.

These unconscious behaviors often reflect unexamined biases. For example, "to be a man or a woman means this, and therefore anything else is strange" (despite gender being socially constructed and changing from culture to culture).

White people are fond of saying they "don't see color, they just see human beings," or of asking us to "not bring race into it." What these people fail to realize is that those very ideas are a luxury. White people don't have to see race because the whole of our culture revolves around whiteness.

Whiteness is the blank canvas, the backdrop. It is the ocean in which drops of water congregate. Blackness and brownness stand out only when they insist that they be noticed in the midst of the sea of whiteness. Or they stand out when they are seen as a threat to this status quo. They are the nails that must be hammered down into the boards of the pier that juts out into the ocean. Or they must be taught a stronger lesson, by being drowned.

To stand out as a Black or brown person in the US is all too often to lose a job, or a child, or a home. To stand out, wanted or not, is all to often to risk death.

Yes, occasionally a Black artist or athlete or even author is allowed to stand out. But that is because they are considered exceptional. White people will often say that these exceptions "transcend race"—because how could something deeply rooted in Black consciousness and culture succeed?

Some white people comprehend this in at least some small way, if they are queer, or disabled, or desperately poor. But as my Black and brown comrades point out, they can never change the color of their skin. There is no way they can hide. So every day means waking up to navigate an unsafe world.

As author and social worker Crystal Blanton says: *"Feeling safe in the world is a privilege. When we navigate our daily lives we should always remember that safety of the mind, the body, the spirit.... It's all relative. Assuming different is oppressive."*

We are complicit in upholding the systems of racism that put so many people in direct danger.

Until we start actively noticing and dismantling white supremacy in all its guises, we are engaging in racist behaviors. Not being actively mean to Black people isn't enough.

Every person can find ways to start dismantling white supremacy. There are more extreme things that we need to be doing in the long run to shift the structure of our society, but for those who have yet to begin, I encourage us to start with one or two of the following, or come up with some of our own:

Dismantling white supremacy starts with noticing our thoughts and assumptions.

It starts with noticing how white people are portrayed on bus shelter ads, in magazines, in movies and books. And then noticing the way Black or brown people are presented, or are absent. With our reading outside our usual boxes. With challenging co-workers on their language, or our bosses on their hiring practices. With questioning the narrative that a Black person "must have done something wrong" when they are killed by the police. With calling out news outlets about biased reporting. With telling the mayor of our town that we disagree with the way policing is done and pledge to do something about it. With listening to the experiences of Black and brown people, and believing what they tell us. With requesting books by Black authors at the library, including in the children's section.

You get the idea.

If white supremacy is all around us, challenging it can be done anywhere, and at any time.

So I would ask all white people this:

Instead of worrying about whether or not we are "a racist," let's undermine white supremacy, every chance we get.

August, 2016

TWENTY-THREE
OMELAS IS HERE
ON KYLE RITTENHOUSE, WHITE SUPREMACY, AND US

"It was not then a question of crime, but rather one of color, that settled a man's conviction on almost any charge."

— *W.E.B. Dubois*

THERE IS no escape from heartbreak. There is no running away from our problems. The small problems, we can change. The large problems are made by interlocking systems that churn on and on and on. They are fueled by human industry, the blood and sweat of working people held under the thumb of oligarchs and plutocrats.

But, as Mario Savio enjoined us to, we can put our bodies on the gears of this machine. And we must.

We must be sand in the gears of the systems that are killing us and choking the planet.

And meanwhile, we must help each other, as often as we can.

THE JUDGE RULED that the AR-15 style firearm Kyle Rittenhouse killed three people with was not a deadly weapon. Rittenhouse loves police. He admires Proud Boys and other white nationalists. He traveled across state lines with this not-a-deadly-weapon, driven there by his mother.

Black men are killed for just existing.

Black women are killed for just existing.

Black children are killed for just existing.

White men? They are considered good for just existing.

Kyle Rittenhouse, a young white man, was acquitted by Judge Bruce Schroeder and coddled by the system that says protestors deserve to be shot and run down in the streets, and that Black, Latine, Asian, and Indigenous lives don't matter at all, except as cannon fodder or minds, hands, and backs that churn out gold and entertainment for the rich.

When a system that kills judges a killer not guilty, what does that say about the society that built it?

A BLACK MAN wandered through a building under construction.

White men wandered through a building under construction.

White women wandered through a building under construction.

White children wandered through a building under construction, taking plywood to build a skateboard ramp.

Only one of these people is dead. His name was Ahmaud Arbery. He was chased and killed by three white men. There are eleven white people on the twelve-person jury. The prosecutor asked that Black pastors supporting Arbery's family be removed from the courtroom.

There is to be no succor for the grieving and oppressed.

WHITE SUPREMACY RUNS rampant through the United States, as in many parts of the globe.

White nationalists crowd school board meetings, intimidating children and parents, screaming—spittle flying from unmasked faces—about sheep.

White nationalists burn torches while shouting, "Jews will not replace us!"

White nationalists hunt down Black men and those who support Black liberation. They spray-paint synagogues. They drive through crowds. They carry guns. Bear mace. Fists.

White men murder Black trans women.

White women call police on Black men out looking at

birds. At Black women who dare to contradict them in public places.

BLACK, Latine, and Indigenous children and adults end up dead simply for playing, or sleeping, or being.

Tamir Rice was playing in a park.

Andy Lopez was playing in an empty lot.

Aiyana Stanley-Jones was sleeping.

Stonechild Chiefstick tripped and fell with a screwdriver. He was shot dead, too.

"WHO WILL PROTECT us if we are robbed, or raped, or murdered?"

Dealing with violent crime is only four percent of police activity in most cities. Mostly, police harass people that wealthy or middle-class white people deem unacceptable. Rich white people close their hearts and their gates.

The systems they uphold close human beings into cages.

INDIGENOUS CHILDREN ARE STILL STOLEN from their homes.

Black children are still stolen from their homes.

Asian grandparents are beaten on the streets.

Indigenous women go missing every day.

People are terrorized in jails, awaiting trial, because they cannot afford bail.

Black people are stopped and fingerprinted because —by going about their lives—they are considered "suspicious."

"IF THE CHILD *were brought up into the sunlight out of that vile place, if it were cleaned and fed and comforted, that would be a good thing indeed; but if it were done, in that day and hour all the prosperity and beauty and delight of Omelas would wither and be destroyed. Those are the terms. To exchange all the goodness and grace of every life in Omelas for that single, small improvement: to throw away the happiness of thousands for the chance of the happiness of one: that would be to let guilt within the walls indeed."*

— *Ursula K. Le Guin*[2]

WHITE PEOPLE:

If you do not insist that Black, brown, Asian, and Indigenous lives matter...

If you do not speak out against injustice...

If you do not actively root out racism within yourself and your communities...

If you do not give up your seat at the table when you figure out the only other people sitting there are white like you...

If you do not make noise. Refuse to move. Throw sand on the gears of this brutal machine...

You may as well pull the trigger yourself next time.

Because none of this is about one "bad" person. Or one "bad" institution. This is about all of us. About every white person breathing right now. About our ancestors and who profited, in large ways or small. This is about the whole filthy system and every stinking, interlocking, rotting piece.

EVERY DEAD BODY was a living person once. Someone loved them. Someone mourns them.

Eleanor Bumpurs. Emmett Till. George Stinney Jr. Loreal Tsingine. Sandra Bland. Kayla Moore.

The twelve million indigenous people killed in the US between 1492 and 1900. The thousands more killed or gone missing since.

The thirty-five million Africans enslaved.

The more than four thousand Chinese workers killed while building railroads.

Their spirits call out for justice. For freedom. For the right to simply live.

WHAT ARE you doing to help bring about change?

Are you fighting for history to be taught in schools?

Are you working with unhoused people toward solutions around food, sanitation, and housing?

Are you speaking out against injustice?

Are you monkey wrenching?

Are you organizing workers?

Are you sharing food and resources?

Are you holding billionaires' feet to the fire?

Are you listening?

Are you...

I'VE WRITTEN these words one hundred times over the past decades. Ideas for engagement. Words calling for us to show up for each other.

So today, I want to hear your ideas.

We can't run away. We can't bury our problems. We can't turn away from suffering.

We cannot escape to faery. We cannot walk away from Omelas, not while Omelas still stands. Not while one child is still tethered in a dark basement, being tortured.

And these days? Any life of relative comfort is built on torture.

What are we doing about it?

"I AM NO LONGER ACCEPTING *the things I cannot change. I am changing the things I cannot accept."*

— Angela Y. Davis

November 2021

TWENTY-FOUR
THE PHOTOGRAPH

My mother died on Winter Solstice. Months later, the family gathered to go through her remaining things. Some costume jewelry, old mementos, and the like.

Among her things were some photographs from my father. Photos from his enlisted days. World War II. Men on military equipment. Men climbing palm trees. Hanging out. Friends at beaches.

Photos I'd never seen before.

My siblings were around me, looking through the assorted objects set out on long tables, going through my mother's other things. In that moment, it was as if I was alone in the room, surrounded by the detritus of a life lived long, lived well. Surrounded by some things that would be treasured, and others that would be thrown away.

Because that's what life is: an odd collection. An assortment of things, only some of which have value to the living. Some of which had value only to yourself. And you're gone now.

Flipping through these photographs, one startled me so much I almost dropped it. It wasn't my father. It wasn't anyone I knew. But it was one of the photos from World War II. From the Pacific theater.

The fading black-and-white picture clearly illustrated some military talent show. A thing to entertain the soldiers in their free time in the midst of a harrowing war. A war that would leave some of them, like my father, alcoholics, not quite recovering from all that they had seen or done.

But I'm dancing around this thing held in my hands. This photograph.

The person on the makeshift stage was a white man. Wearing black face.

I almost dropped it. I wanted to rip the photograph in two. I wanted to burn it.

I wanted to hide it. Reshuffle it into a pile of photos my siblings were unlikely to go through. And then I paused. Took a breath. And I realized I had to take that photo home with me.

I had to stare it in the face. This horror, this mockery, because it too was part of my legacy. This racism. This casual dismissal of another human's life. Of their dignity.

I needed to make sure I knew that along with the photos I keep on my ancestor altar I didn't forget this one. Because...

Even though it wasn't my father, it was someone he knew. And he cared enough about that photo, at one time in his life, to save it. He found the comedy sketch at some talent show in the middle of hell—this enlisted friend of his in black face—humorous enough to have kept that image.

Even though I was sure he had forgotten it in the decades that followed, at one point in my father's life the picture meant something to him.

And that sort of racism is part of me too.

Even though I fight for justice. Even though I stand with the families and friends of those killed by the police. Even though yes, some of my best friends are Black. The buildup of hundreds of years of systemic oppression and racist assumptions are still there.

I hate to think that things flow in my blood, because that's its own sort of eugenics-leaning racist trope.

And yet things *do* flow through a family's understanding and shared experiences. Like our childhood name for Brazil nuts. Calling them something so vile I won't repeat it. Who taught us that?

My mother insisted she never taught us to be racist, or to treat people differently. And yet my family is full of the sort of casual, unconscious racism that infects far too many white Americans. An ordinary racism. Not foaming at the mouth. Not directly violent. Just...opinions that prop up systems of inequity and injustice. Opinions that kill slowly, over time.

If a brown or Black person showed up for dinner, we would welcome them with open arms. Every last member of my immediate blood family.

But a large portion of my family also says things about people on welfare. Even though we were on food stamps for part of my childhood, "that was different." That was us. We weren't taking advantage of the system.

And a large portion of my family says things about immigrants, even though they often work alongside them. Well, but those immigrants have learned how to become legal so they're okay. They're not like those other people.

A large portion of my family says things about Muslims, and when I counter that, they say that of course they don't mean *every* Muslim.

A large portion of my family says a lot of things.

And I've argued with them for years, off and on. Taking breaks when the shouting grew too hard, then coming back again.

Just like I argued with my father, starting at around age thirteen. About the fact that there was no such thing as "Asian drivers" and that mentioning that they were Asian in that context was racist. He insisted, "No. That's not racist. They just drive that way in their own country." Because they surely weren't Americans. And they didn't know any better.

It wasn't anything *bad* that he was saying. It's never anything bad.

But all of this casual, banal sort of racism is bad enough. It props up harm and eruptions of hatred.

In my adopted city, just like my former home, police kill young Black men for reasons that are never reason enough. And in my adopted city, two young Black and Muslim women were just terrorized by a white man on a train. And three other white men stood to defend these young women. Two are dead now. One is recovering from his injuries. Turns out the killer had assaulted a Black woman just days before.

And near my former city, a white man killed a black

man over a political argument on the bus. And in Maryland, a young Black man was killed for not stepping off the sidewalk. And in my former city, the coffee shop where I used to sit and write—a worker-owned collective of ragtag beautiful young people of all races and genders, but largely people of color—more than once have had their windows smashed by white supremacists.

And in my adopted city last week, racists gathered, insisting they were only there in support of love and free speech. It wasn't about hatred. It's never about hatred. Except for when it all too suddenly is.

And all of this connects and traces back to that photograph. That one photograph in a pile of so many others unnoticed, unwanted, hidden away, neglected. Not out of shame. But because people had forgotten it was even there.

Or perhaps they didn't want to look.

Until we dismantle the lie of white supremacy in all its guises, our communities will continue to be broken, and ripped apart.

So I'm not going to forget it's there. I'm going to remember to look at this hideous photograph, this piece of history, and then I'm going to look into my heart every day.

And I'm going to question my assumptions. And every day, I'm going to show up again.

And try to fight.

June, 2017

TWENTY-FIVE
I WAS A SOCIAL JUSTICE ASSHOLE:
OR HOW I LEARNED TO HATE WHITE SUPREMACY

White supremacy is everywhere. We are bathing in it. We breathe it. We eat it. It surrounds us. There is no escaping it.

Like all other forms of self-absorption, white supremacy means we never have to consider anyone else's viewpoint. We never have to notice what the world might feel like from someone else's experience. Because, in our self-absorption, we assume that our experience is universal.

Our jokes are everyone's jokes. Our pathos is everyone's pathos. Our lies are everyone's lies.

Except they aren't.

And we're assholes. Unwitting assholes, but assholes just the same.

What's the difference between run-of-the-mill, garden variety self-absorption and white supremacy?

White supremacy kills a lot more people.

Through suicide. Crushing poverty. Incarceration. Package bombs on door steps. Hiring discrimination.

Redlining. Lead paint. Assumption of guilt. Government supplied crack cocaine. Educational disparity. Heart disease. Diabetes. Bullets. Firebombs. Despair.

WHITE SUPREMACY TELLS us that white people are beautiful.

White supremacy tells us that white people are smart.

White supremacy tells us that white people work harder.

White supremacy tells us that white people are more trustworthy.

White supremacy tells us that white people are… superior.

WHITE *SUPREMACISTS* CROW about white superiority. They carry tiki torches in midnight marches. They burn churches. They administer beatings. Some of them burn crosses.

THE REST OF US? We smugly say "We're not like them." We'll even say we don't believe in the superiority of whiteness.

SOME of even actively fight to counter white supremacy.

. . .

BUT ITS INFLUENCE still creeps in. And how could it not? White supremacy is everywhere, and it forms our comfort zone. A nice buffer between ourselves and the rest of the world.

AND THAT COMFORTABLE BUFFER –that barely conscious belief system– is killing people. All the things that keep white people comfortable drain the life away from everyone else.

SOMETIMES ITS SLOW death from a thousand micro-aggressions. The constant chipping away at self-esteem, the constant questioning, the asking for an explanation that you never listen to, the hair touching, the dismissal, the rewriting, whitewashing, and erasure of history. The constant asking of "can't you take a joke?"

OTHER TIMES it's a 17 year old cellist and honor student opening his front door and being blown to bits. Or a teen asking for directions to school getting shot at.

Other times it's Trayvon Martin not making it home from the store. Or it's Emmett Till. Or Oscar Grant. Or Alan Blueford. Or Kayla Moore. Or Yuvette Henderson. Or Larnelle Bruce. Or Rekia Boyd. Or Sandra Bland. Or all the women raped by Daniel Holtzclaw. Or Quanice Hayes. Or Sarah Lee Circle Bear. Or Mesha Caldwell.

KNOWING I'd be brain dead en route home from teaching at a conference, I downloaded an old film I liked – Easy A – one that I'd found clever and funny. Then I noticed that there was a stupid, fucking, racist joke embedded in it.

Aw shucks.

So much white-made art hides those loaded package bombs.

Like the gleeful recitation of the poem, The Congo, in the oh-so-touching Dead Poet's Society.

Like books written in the 21st century that still reference "darkest Africa" or "swarthy complexions" or "inscrutable eyes," or "exotic looks." Or Asians who know martial arts or get all As. Or Muslims who are terrorists. Or Black kids who are abandoned by drug addicted mothers. Or Indian women, all versed in the Kama Sutra.

ONCE YOU SEE THIS, or hear it, or perceive it, you can't not perceive it anymore.

AND HOPEFULLY, you can't not see the way all of this leads directly to twelve year old Tamir Rice –or thirteen year old Andy Lopez– being shot dead because they had the temerity to play, just like white children play.

. . .

OR THAT IT also leads to cluster bombs being dropped on brown children in countries no longer so far away. Because we perceive brown people as inherently more of a threat than white people.

BECAUSE THEY THREATEN our concept of white supremacy.

I WANT to talk about this centering of whiteness and why I was a social justice asshole. I'm not going to detail my past sins of racist bullshit, which are many. I want to center on my more recent activism.

I'VE BEEN an activist since my teens. I thought I was committed to the cause, although for a long time I was more focused on peace than on justice. That's okay. It was all I knew. We all need to learn.

I thought I knew that love was the answer and we needed to treat people as individuals and yes, work for justice and an end to class disparity, state violence, and war.

For a brief interlude, I also thought that Occupy Oakland having "Fuck the Police" marches was a bit much.

Luckily, that didn't last long.

And then, once I figured out that not only Occupy, but Black and Latinx and Indigenous people in Oakland had every right to say "fuck the police," I started doing something about it.

Except, some of the time, I was doing it wrong.

A GROUP of white interfaith folks met once a month to read the names of those killed by police in California in front of the Oakland Police department. This was a list I spent hours of time compiling, and that I shared with whomever asked for it.

That was a good thing.

We also showed up to protest the militarization of police. We blockaded and risked arrest. We showed up to support the families of those killed by police, at courthouses, the state capitol, and City Hall.

That was also a good thing.

BUT I WILL NEVER FORGET, that at two events protesting extrajudicial killings, and mourning the dead, I had been asked to bring those lists of names of the dead... and arrived, thinking I would be the one to read those names. At least some of them.

THAT WAS HIGHLY INCORRECT.

I STILL HADN'T FIGURED out that there was no fucking way I –a white person– should be on the mic in the middle of a group of Black and Latinx people.

Despite being used to being on the mic in other communities. Despite having compiled those lists, and all the other things.

Because, though my heart ached and I was filled with fury, though I had been showing up, *I was not the one at risk*. My family was safe. Yes, some of my dear friends were on the firing line...but I was not. And I never would be.

I had to realize that I was still centering whiteness. Thank all the Gods and Goddesses there were amazing, strong, fierce, and patient Black and Latinx people in leadership that I was privileged to work with. They looked me in the eye, thanked me for the list, then gave the list –and the microphone– to someone else.

I gave those lists over and also learned to uncenter myself a few degrees more, and to step back.

I learned to show up at meetings and not be in leadership.

I learned how to listen. Again. And again.

AND I'M STILL MAKING mistakes. Still centering myself. But I also listen a little better now.

UNLEARNING and dismantling white supremacy within myself will probably take my lifetime.

DISMANTLING white supremacy in society will take generations.

WHERE AM I heading with all of these threads? Back where I began: White supremacy is everywhere. We live in it. We breathe in it. Currently? There's almost no escaping it.

AND…

EVERY SINGLE DAY, we have the opportunity to notice.

Every single day, we have the chance to point out the operations and expressions of white supremacy, to ourselves and to others.

Every day, we have the opportunity to have the conversations. To change our own self-expression. To ask non-marginalized artists and writers and film makers to do better. To do the work necessary to begin dismantling systems of oppression and terror based on the assumption of white supremacy and on Black and brown laziness, ineffectiveness, and self-inflicted poverty.

WHAT ELSE CAN WE DO? We can support art that is not centered on whiteness and white supremacy. We can amplify the vision and voices of more marginalized communities. We can pay Black and brown and indigenous people what they are worth. We can question mostly white "best of" lists. We can insist that conferences increase the percentage of non-white speakers.

I COULD CONTINUE LISTING possible action items for another page but know that humans are resourceful. Once we start noticing how the world really works, and how white supremacy really operates?

We can each come up with a list of our own.

WE CAN STOP BEING ASSHOLES, invoke some empathy, compassion, and outrage, and get to work.

April, 2018

TWENTY-SIX

REPARATIONS ARE NOT ENOUGH

"The major sources of wealth for most of the super rich are inheritances and in life transfers. The big reason is racial differences in access to resources to transfer to the next generation." – William Darity

---

"The top 10% of families own 75.3% of the nation's wealth. The bottom half of families own 1.1% of it. The families squished in between those two groups own 24.6% of the national wealth."

– Matt Bruenig

. . .

The need for reparations for African and Native Americans is real.

It is also not enough.

THIS TOPIC IS on my mind and heart a lot lately because of things I witness in my communities and in the lives of friends.

THESE THINGS FILL me with anger, as they should.

THE NEED FOR REPARATIONS, and for truth, and perhaps eventually, a long time from now, for some sort of reconciliation, are tied to the history of oppression and dehumanization that infiltrates our society today.

THE RAMIFICATIONS OF RACISM, white supremacy, bigotry, wealth-hoarding, and entrenched systems of inequity mean that we cannot simply say "slavery ended a long time ago."

WE CANNOT SIMPLY SAY "Native Americans should just leave the reservation if they don't like it."

. . .

THERE IS NO "GETTING OVER IT", when one lives within systems of oppression, even when one lives a relatively happy and successful life.

INSTEAD OF BLACK, or Latinx, or First Nations people "getting over it," how about white people increase our awareness of the oppressive systems at play, and do something to change our society's values?

IN THE UNITED STATES, wealth is measured by property, education, assets, and money.

1,400 AMERICANS CONTROL MOST of the wealth in the US. These are the .01%.

THE .01% own exponentially more assets than the top 1%.

THE TOP 1% are predominantly white.

WHITE PEOPLE DON'T CONTROL MOST of the wealth because they are smarter or work harder. White people control most of the wealth because of systematic oppression, white supremacy, and the continued impact of personal bias, and racist policies.

ALSO, when systems are set up to disenfranchise whole sectors of a population – and keep them from educational opportunities, voting, internships, funding, housing, loans – there are almost no avenues available for wealth accrual.

AND UNDER CAPITALISM, wealth and property accrual are the only things that seem to matter.

OUT OF 540 billionaires in the US, two are African American.

ACCRUING MONEY and land does nothing to help the soul.

HOWEVER, access to basic resources makes day to day life much easier and less stressful.

STRESS CAUSES HEALTH PROBLEMS. Lack of resources also leads to extreme lack of time. Lack of time leads to difficulty in taking care of the most basic of life's needs.

ASTONISHINGLY, even under crushing circumstances, creativity rises, a testament to spirit.

A BLACK WOMAN'S son was murdered by white supremacists in 2016. She now struggles to care for her remaining son in the aftermath of this horror. Her hours at work keep getting cut. Her son needs medicine and food.

WHERE DOES SHE TURN? Where is the safety net for unexpected murder from a hate crime?

IN 1921, white people rioted in Tulsa, Oklahoma, smashing Black-owned businesses and setting fire to the district known as "Black Wall Street."

THIS DEALT a significant blow to the attempts at the process of reconstruction after the close of the American Civil War, setting back the ability of African Americans to accrue any sort of financial stability.

. . .

IT ALSO ENSURED that Black Americans would continue to live under the constant threat of violence.

BLACK AMERICANS ARE EXPECTED to toe the line. Simply being Black in America puts one's life at risk.

AFRICAN AMERICAN WOMEN are now the most highly educated group in the United States.

IT DOESN'T MATTER.

A BLACK WOMAN took on student loan debt in order to garner the advanced degree that would enable her to serve her community. She and her partner work hard, only just making enough money – her at the career that required this degree, him also working with underserved populations – to pay student loans, feed their children, and pay the rent.

THERE IS NO SAVING MONEY. There is no accrual of assets. The children will not inherit anything other than keen minds, creativity, and a parent's love.

NO FREED slave ever got the promised "forty acres and a mule" that would have enabled them to scratch out a living and enjoy the benefits of property afforded white Americans.

There was nothing to pass on to children other than hard labor.

EDUCATION WAS SEGREGATED and often not available at all.

NATIVE AMERICAN CHILDREN were taken from their families and forced into schools that stripped them of both culture and community.

BANKS WOULD NOT LEND money to Black citizens. There was no way to buy property.

WHEN MONEY WAS FINALLY LENT, it was at extortionist rates, and homes or businesses could only be purchased in certain "redlined" neighborhoods.

. . .

ONCE THOSE NEIGHBORHOODS became homes to Black communities, they were often either torn down, or slated for "urban renewal."

ONCE URBAN RENEWAL OCCURRED, the very families who built those neighborhoods were shoved out, fracturing communities and undermining their abilities to accrue equity.

AS RENTS RISE, displacing more and more people, Black and Latinx neighborhoods become increasingly white.

THE UNITED STATES government stole more than 1.5 billion acres of land from First Nations tribes.

TREATIES WERE WRITTEN AND BROKEN.

BLACK AND NATIVE families have forever being forced to start from scratch, whereas even working-poor white families tend to have more access to resources and education or even modest wealth, such as having a car passed down, or getting help with rent in times of extreme need.

THE VOTING RIGHTS ACT, which was fought for with blood and ink, has been gutted. Voter disenfranchisement, redistricting, poll taxes, and capricious Voter ID laws ensure that Black families are often locked out of the very processes that govern their lives.

BLACK AMERICANS ARE INCARCERATED at an alarmingly high rate, which is the direct result of "colorblind" racist judicial systems. The War on Drugs, Stop and Frisk, and Broken Windows policing all contribute to the inequitable treatment of Black, Latinx, and Native Americans, and further disenfranchisement.

ANGRY YET? Or are you arguing with me in your head?

REPARATIONS ARE NECESSARY, but they are not enough.

Those of us less affected by these realities need to become angry.

Then we need to agitate for real change.

BY 2023, every Black and Native adult should receive a basic minimum income of at least $1000 each month.

EVERY BLACK and Native person in the US should receive free education and health care.

WE CAN START with these populations, and then move on to others.

AS FOR THE PERSONAL LEVEL?

WHITE PEOPLE CAN LOOK at what we can do to make reparations of our own: Pay off school lunch debts. Fund Black run organizations. Volunteer. Work to change local voting and housing policies. Work on police, court, and prison reform or – my preference – abolition.

WE MUST WORK DILIGENTLY to change every interlocking oppressive system at play.

We must work diligently to undermine white supremacy.

We must offer more than lip service to equity, justice, and love.

WE MUST GROW ANGRY ENOUGH, and feel enough fierce love, to say "enough."

July, 2017

TWENTY-SEVEN
SOMETIMES WE NEED A BATTLE CRY

Unless you comprehend the lives of others, some of their words or actions may feel strange. They may even run counter to your very reasonable beliefs and practices.

And then one day you see. Or hear. And your well-ordered sense of reason is blown into one thousand pieces, and scattered by the wind.

You are left within the burning rubble of your comprehension, and from within the piles of stone, you see a world you never could perceive before.

PANTHEACON, 2016. One hundred and thirty people crowded in a ballroom circle, talking about pain, and fear, and grief, and inequity. Talking about why Black Lives Matter. Working the ways of restorative justice.

Near the close of this "Restorative Justice: Black Lives Matter" workshop, I began a drum beat. I had asked the white people in the circle to let the Black and brown people in the room start the vocalizations and rhythms, to lay the foundation for our weaving.

Body rhythm started. Then a voice, chanting "freedom." Other voices added, building. Dancers moved into the center. Voices swelled and shifted, the rhythms built, one on top of the other. The room filled up with music. And then, weaving itself over what we had established, came another voice, a louder voice, chanting "No justice! No peace!"

Others joined this voice, high and low, soft and strong. "No justice! No peace!" Underneath it all, the call of freedom continued. The rhythm built.

And built.

And built.

Until we all turned toward the center, concentric clumps of moving bodies and raised voices shifting to a vast tone, as we sent our cries up and out into the world.

This was a beautiful, powerful thing.

Afterward, a white man approached me to ask a question. He'd needed to step back from the energy raising, because he didn't want to be sending "no justice, no peace" out as a prayer, as a spell, as a working of magic. He didn't want to invoke a lack of peace and justice.

This makes good sense. We are often taught: don't phrase things in the negative. And: make sure to be careful what exactly you call in.

I paused a moment and replied, "The phrase is short hand for 'If there is no justice, there will be no peace.'" I also said that I had made sure we ended with strong toning, letting the words drop away into pure sound. He said he was able to step back in for that.

There was more I wanted to say, but I could feel others wanting to step up and speak, to have a moment. So I let it go.

Part of me wished I hadn't. There was so much more to the conversation than we even began to touch upon.

Because, you see, if we were only thinking magically, he was mostly right. We want—mostly—to state clearly to the cosmos and our Gods exactly what we want to bring about. What we want to conjure. What we want to draw in.

But if we were thinking from the places in the rubble, staring up at whole new swaths of sky, if we only *saw* and *felt* the lives our siblings who are different from us *actually* lead...the very magic that we make would change.

We would see that sometimes what we need to conjure is the power to get things done, and the insistence that we will let no person, faction, or force stand in our way.

I'm not calling this man out. He was clearly thoughtful, and a person of good will. I just want us all—particularly those who are any combination of white, able bodied, middle class, fill in your own blank—to pause and think:

"What magic might be necessary to tear down the old world in order to build anew?"

I've been involved in peace and justice work since my early teens. But until I began forging closer ties to Black and non-Black people of color, I could not clearly *see* the brutal conditions of their ordinary day-to-day. The constant conditions of racism, disenfranchisement, and inequity.

Worse, I couldn't *feel* any of that. And the feeling of it, the slap in the face or the grinding down of depression or the high blood pressure brought about by simply getting along in a world that tells your children they are animals and tells you that you are neither beautiful nor smart...that feeling is what we need sometimes to recognize that nice magic, kind magic, the magic of drawing things in, is not enough.

Sometimes we need a battle cry.

Sometimes we need to shout at the top of our lungs a clear statement to the powers that be and say, "As long as there is not justice here, we will hound you, we will harry you, we will dog your heels, day and night, and you will have no peace."

Sometimes our magic is a declaration of our power.

Sometimes our magic is both a blessing and curse.

Sometimes our magic tells the world exactly where we stand.

And when we are dealing with issues of justice? When the Black and brown people in the room are stepping to the front—as they should—I'm damn well going to follow their lead.

March, 2016

With deep gratitude to Crystal Blanton, who teaches me Restorative Justice and led the circle with me, and to Katrina Messenger, who began the "freedom" chant, and to Beverley Smith, who shouted "No justice, no peace!"

and to everyone else who spoke and sang and pounded feet that day. And to all my comrades who weave the words of magic and do the work of justice, every day.

This Restorative Justice circle happened at Pantheacon, a large Pagan and Polytheist conference in San Jose, California. Crystal and I also led an RJ circle at the Parliament of the World's Religions and have continued this practice at other conferences.

TWENTY-EIGHT
DISTURBING THE PEACE

I used to be a great proponent of peace.

My prayers and meditations were often aimed in that direction. My actions, too, to the best of my ability, as I marched in the streets, wrote letters, and examined my own anger and violence.

The killing of Oscar Grant in 2009, and the killing of Alan Blueford in 2012 –and all of those brutalized and killed by police in between and since– changed my relationship with peace. Vigiling and marching with families whose loved ones were stolen by police violence has shifted my view. Organizing with Black leaders and communities of color affected by police militarization and systemic harassment and imprisonment has diminished my talk of peace.

But why? Why isn't the concept of peace just as important as it always has been? Here are some reasons why: Talk of peace can be used to stifle anger. Talk of peace can serve to calm us down. Talk of peace all too often fails to become talk of justice. Talk of peace can all too often wish to rush toward niceness, toward a balance that doesn't exist, and toward a veneer that will soon crack.

Before there can be peace, there must be justice.

Before there can be justice, there must be truth. And some of us must learn better to listen.

Do I think peace is bad? Do I think that the endless wars being waged around the world are good? No. I don't. But it seems to me that talk of peace is premature. We do not just cease war and fighting. First, we listen. Then we tell the truth. Then we work toward justice. When people have justice, they liberate one another. When people have justice, they build systems of equity. When people have justice...there comes a possibility for peace.

"No justice, no peace!"

As a rallying cry for liberation this means "Until there is justice in our communities – economic justice, environmental justice, racial justice, gender justice – we will continue to upset you and to disturb your sense of peace."

"No justice, no peace!" This is also a simple statement of reality: without justice, the concept of peace is meaningless.

The roots of war are watered by injustice.

Focusing on peace without working for justice feels like we want humans to just wake up one morning and miraculously get along. As if a spiritual awakening alone will make everything better. Spiritual awakenings can help, don't get me wrong. But spiritual awakenings can either help us look at suffering more deeply or enable us to forget that suffering exists at all.

In Dr. King's great speech against the war in Vietnam he spoke of the triplets of racism, militarism, and extreme materialism. These are ever with us. No matter what our spiritual path is, we can find practices to counter all of these. We do not begin on a global scale. We begin as individuals. We begin in our communities. We can continuously seek the roots of racism, militarism, and materialism within ourselves and all our thoughts and choices.

We can start the work over, every single day, to choose and foster justice.

We do this as beings motivated by love. Once we choose to work for justice, we can begin to imagine what peace might actually look like.

I leave you with with ten possible practices toward justice. They are simple. They are one way to begin.

Ten Practices Toward Justice

1. Listen deeply.
2. Examine your assumptions.
3. Study the systems in play.
4. Amplify the voices of those most affected by injustice.
5. Challenge yourself and others.
6. Tell the harder truths.
7. Seek equity in your communities.

8. Listen deeply.
9. Organize (keeping in mind #4).
10. Disturb the peace.

January, 2015

PART 5

WE'RE HERE, WE'RE QUEER

TWENTY-NINE

TRIGGER WARNINGS

THE NEW BELLE ÉPOQUE IS KILLING MY FRIENDS

La Belle Époque: The era between approximately 1870 and the outbreak of World War I.

It was an age of great scientific and technological breakthrough, from automobiles, to telephones, to cinema, airplanes, radioactivity, germ theory, and vaccines.

Another mark of the Golden Age was artistic and cultural fecundity. Post-Impressionism, Fauvism, Modernism, Expressionism, Cubism, Abstraction, The Beaux-Arts, the Pre-Raphaelites, Art Nouveau architecture, the Jugendstil Movement, Literary Realism, Naturalism, and Symbolism were all active movements during this time.

An age of great economic prosperity and wealth, the Belle Époque was built upon colonialism, imperialism, and a massive income and class disparity reliant on cheap labor and increased physical distances between the ultra-wealthy, the working classes, and the poor.

We are living in a New Golden Age.

. . .

THE NEW BELLE Époque is killing my friends.

It is killing the friends of my friends. The Golden Age is killing the friends and loved ones of people I've never even met.

This Golden Age of the super wealthy, the glitterati, the politicians, the multi-billionaires thieving from those who sleep in their cars because they don't have time to go back to their apartments between the three jobs they hold in order to stay alive...

This New Belle Époque kills families with drone strikes. It kills factory workers in Pakistan and schoolchildren in Flint and Portland. It kills women in Owsley County and Dakar and men in Oakland and Dubai. It kills teachers and nurses and men and women walking home from work. It kills through high blood pressure, and poverty, and racism, and misogyny.

The New Belle Époque has very long arms.

The left arm reaches out a hand to grab and snatch while the right holds up a gilded and perfumed fan that shields eyes from the effects of its own actions, its inactions, its corruption, narcissism, and its greed.

But I'm talking about none of that.

When I say the New Belle Époque is killing my friends, I'm pointing to the secondary effects of living under the crushing weight and struggle of being Black, or brown, or trans, or queer, or poor, or sensitive, or any combination of the above.

The New Belle Époque is causing my friends to sacrifice their own lives on the altars of despair.

Placing stones into her pockets, setting her cane and hat by the river bed, Virginia Woolf walked into the water.

She had lived through La Belle Époque, and World War I.

At the dawn of World War II, her home bombed twice, Woolf was hearing voices again.

She struggled with depression. In the advent of a second cataclysm, the water was already rising around her, it was almost over her head.

Woolf declared, "I feel that I am going mad again. I feel we can't go through another of those terrible times."

She was speaking of herself, and to her husband, Leonard. Yet one wonders what may have happened had not the larger times, the epoch of the world, felt so crushing on top of her other troubles.

What is outside of us puts pressure on what is within.

I KNOW. Depression lies. Depression kills. Mental illness stalks communities, and we never know when it will take a loved one or co-worker away.

These recent suicides of activists and artists—of genderqueer psychic painters and performers, of street warriors fighting for justice—might have happened anyway, no matter what.

Yet I can't help but feel that the tension all of us live with right now hurried these bright spirits on their way.

Perhaps if the pressure to just pay rent was not so great...

Perhaps if being trans or Black or brown or femme was not to be a target of violence, disgust, or disregard...

Perhaps if there was a greater appreciation of beauty, difference, justice, and joy...

Perhaps...if we had been allowed to build the world we wanted, instead of spending all our time on making money, and all our money on making weapons of war—or paying for another set of bloody diamonds for the necks of the ultra rich—my friends would have found some room to breathe and be.

The New Belle Époque is killing my friends.

The .0001% have blood all over their hands. They bathe in it. Every. Single. Day.

The terror of the situation is this: they force us to bathe in blood, too. Our faces are spattered with it. It is in every cheap piece of clothing we buy, and in every strawberry picked by fingers other than ours.

In order to live, we are forced to eat our own.

Allen Ginsberg's Moloch still devours us all. The jaws of global capitalism and war grind us all down.

The only ones who sleep well at night—I imagine—are those who don't worry how their children will get to school in the morning, or if their loved ones will make it home alive.

The rest of us? We either worry directly about the day to day, or we worry for our friends who live more precariously than we do ourselves. We either worry about getting enough food to eat, or we worry that we are killing those who give us access to our food. Or we worry that we will be hounded to death because of our differences, or smothered by neglect.

For anyone trying to carve out space in this world while creating the world we want to come...sometimes it is overwhelming. It feels like the floodwaters are rising, sweeping away supports, tugging the mind and body downward until a person drowns.

Sometimes—despite plans for a new performance, or having gotten all the art together for an exhibit, despite a party being planned in our honor, or friends wishing us happy birthday, despite being lauded for our activism in the news—sometimes we take our lives out of this world, to someplace that feels safer, more welcoming, less stressful, less hateful, less frightening, less fraught.

Sometimes the unknown is far less frightening than the known.

It is said that after cataclysms and disasters, suicide rates rise.

For all but the wealthiest and most sheltered, this Golden Age is an ongoing state of cataclysm and disaster.

In the United States today, suicide rates among people of color are higher than those of white people. More men commit suicide than women. Trans people are at higher risk for suicide than cis people.

People who are rejected by families or lack social support are at greatest risk for suicide.

People who are discriminated against are at high risk for suicide.

People with physical or sexual abuse histories have increased risk of suicide.

People with intersections of discrimination or abuse are at the highest risk for suicide.

In the New Belle Époque, Black activists are resorting to suicide on courthouse steps or in their homes. Trans performance artists resort to suicide. Queer painters resort to suicide. Poor people resort to suicide. Farmers in India resort to suicide.

There is something called "minority stress." It is a byproduct of this Golden Age we live in.

And this Golden Age is killing my friends.

We do not have to continue to uphold this twisted world.

We must find ways to dance and dare with one another.

We must find ways to feed and nurture and protect each other.

We must find ways to live.

October, 2016

THIRTY
I WILL DIE LOVING YOU

I wasn't even yet sure enough to call myself queer. But queer I was.

"Are you a boy or a girl?" The repeated calling out of my childhood.

And then the androgynous ties, striped purple, black, and silver, so narrow on my button-down shirts. Men's suits, I wore. My body swam in them. And 1950s party frocks festooned with chains and cinched in with leather.

So. Much. Anger.

Slamming doors open with my feet. Swaggering through into Southern California sunlight. Everyone else thought I was a dyke. I was, but didn't really know it yet.

I hadn't kissed a girl. Not really. Sort of.

But yes, I'd been in love.

With my best friend. A girl who drove us through the twilit streets of LA.

Rejected by boys—over and over—as too weird, too aggressive, too damn smart. Targeted by men since before I could comprehend. The moment I first noticed, I was twelve (though there'd been earlier times). Told that this man would like to carpet a floor with mirrors, and have me walk across them in a miniskirt.

Then I was thirteen years old, at a cast party for our local community theater. I was told I shouldn't tempt older men.

Men pressed their lips against my freshly tightened braces, and their hands against my breasts.

I was a virgin. Whatever the fuck that matters, or that means. Until I was eighteen.

I hung out with the gay boys when I dropped out of high school for community college at sixteen. We were flamboyantly theatrical, each in our own way. We'd go to gay bars in Los Angeles. The only places that would let us in, despite our ages.

The only places our mixed crew could be.

We danced. Oh, how we danced. Some of my friends were joyful. Some were so afraid. But we were there.

At eighteen, I moved north, to San Francisco, from the smog to the fog.

Men were dying, everywhere. Sarcoma lesions like plum islands on their skin.

Marching from the Castro to City Hall, holding our candles. Chanting "Harvey Milk and George Moscone!" Martyrs, dead not quite a decade, but fresh in the minds of this city. We were a sea of light in darkness and they were our guides. When we reached the dome, and the rows of pollarded trees, so lumpy and misshapen, Sister Boom Boom's voice rose on the bullhorn, whispering sharply in the night,

"The word came down from Washington. Let them die!"

I wept.

Maud's. Amelia's. The dimly lit lesbian bars of San Francisco, long since gone. Pussies in Pajamas singing silly songs. I asked old-school butches to dance. They were so hot I could barely stand it, in their crisp shirts and tight jeans. Filled with my desire, I'd broken the rules. They were the ones who were supposed to be asking me.

Beautiful women intimidated me. It was easier to be with men. To swagger and kiss. To stomp my boots and ride my motorcycle. To ask for dates and get them.

But there were women, even so. Gorgeous, all of them, because of who they were. Butch and femme. And some men as queer as me. Black men in miniskirts and lipstick. White men in dandy outfits. Nerds in glasses who discussed philosophy.

Dancing in a mirrored box filled with naked women, as small windows rose and fell, fell and rose. I would crouch down to the glass. "Who's your favorite ecstatic poet?" I would ask. One man came in to discuss science fiction in the seconds between songs. He left me a hardbound copy of *V for Vendetta*.

All too fitting, even still.

Queer Nation taking over bars and slapping neon stickers everywhere. Queer magazines abounded: *Taste of Latex. Frighten the Horses. RFD.*

I kissed my girlfriend goodbye on the sidewalk, getting ready to put my helmet on and hop on my black motorcycle, festooned with glowing stars. A small convertible GT backed up, knocking into my bike. My girlfriend and I broke our kiss. It had been a mistake. A slipped clutch. Right? The car backed up again. Then again. Revving and backing. Revving and backing. Shoving the metal bike against our flesh.

I was confused, and fought to keep the bike upright. My girlfriend attacked, screaming at the man, and kicked her powerful, tiny feet against his car. He—and the woman with him—drove away.

Years later, I married a man. Not sure if I could go to Pride that year. Was I allowed?

Young men strung up in the desert. Trans women killed. And killed. And killed.

I dated, some, per our agreement, but only while I was out of town. A woman. A man. All too rarely. I was learning things, but missing others. My hair was clipped to nonexistence. I wore loose men's jeans. Singlet T-shirts. My tattooed arms hoisted large pots at the soup kitchen. I scrubbed mountains of potatoes. Wrote a book. Went back to school.

Gender non-conforming. That's what they call it now.

Marriage ended. Back with women. Back with men. Practicing packing a cock, both soft in trousers for going out, and hard for the mostly naked, panting, shoving, kissing, leather harness thrusting itself outward on the bed.

Back at queer bars and Goth clubs. Leather pants or corsets, always the plumage of shadows. Of beauty and darkness. Of the need for bodies moving in their joy.

Every sweaty corner was a refuge. Every pulse of light a prayer. Every song a cry of passion to the world.

Years rolled by. Trans marches with my sweetheart, her feet aching in high heels. Concerts with my girlfriend. Brunches with my partner. Politics and wine. Meditation on the streets. Books. Justice. A march for Chelsea Manning. And for too many shot down. Arrested with queer clergy bearing witness to the violence of police.

We are a family, my partners and me. You cannot tell us otherwise. We make a home, each with our separate, introverted space. Two men. One woman. Though one man and one woman are not quite a man, or woman. Not really. We can pass, sometimes. Sometimes not. But the shine is always there. The strangeness. Even the one be-suited heterosexual among us gets called "Lady" sometimes.

"Boy or girl?"

"Straight or gay?"

Queer is the only word to define us. Queer is the word we will wear. And an ocean of strange friends that we call family ebb and flow around us. All making up their families as best as they can, too.

And another year follows yet another day. Checking in after morning prayers, there is word from a beloved friend: There's been a mass shooting. His friends go to that club. One still unaccounted for. He is bereft.

A day of grief shatters a month of joy. A month set aside to mark the uprising, a riot where trans women led gay men to say, "Enough!"

Enough harassment. Enough beatings. Enough killings. Enough arrests. Enough denials of housing. Of children. Of jobs. Of health care. Of being with our loved ones. Enough. Enough. Enough.

We too say enough.

You will not kill us. A few may fall, cut down, but you cannot kill us all. We will not let you. And we will not let you use our blood to organize more hatred and more war. Yes. I'm looking at you. And you. And you, too.

Tonight, I made a decision. It is one I've made before:

I don't want to, but if I have to, I will die in the streets defending my siblings from harm. Be they cis or trans. Black, brown, or white. Men or women. Not men, not women. Queer or straight. Or something wholly new. A parent defending a child. A band of Pagans. A Muslim at prayer. A young black man just hanging out. Two women, white, or brown, kissing on a sidewalk. Comrades locking down. A group of friends dancing and laughing, drinking beer at 1 a.m.

Whether that harm comes from a bigot backed up by an army, a police force, or wielding a single gun. Whether that harm comes from elected officials, or heads of churches, or demagogues spreading lies. Whether that harm comes from a community, slinging words of dismissal or hate.

Or whether that harm comes from one person, pumped full of vitriol by others so fearful, so greedy, so angry, they've forgotten what it is like to love and be loved.

No matter what: I will die loving you, my brothers, sisters, and siblings. Whether that is fifty years from now, or five years, or today.

We are fierce. We are tender. We are weak and strong. We shatter the doors of City Hall or we can't get out of bed.

We are beautiful. Remember that.

I'm willing to die for you, my friends, but I'd rather live. I'd rather you lived, too.

As my comrade Elena Rose so eloquently puts it: "It's still a world with plums in it, my loves, & chamomile & lipstick & cellos. It's still a world with us in it. Find a hand & hold on."

And as I say, all too often, and I mean it every time:

Stay safe. Stay strong. Stay in love.

June, 2016

THIS ESSAY WAS WRITTEN PARTIALLY *in response to the Pulse murders in Orlando, Florida.*

THIRTY-ONE
SEXISM IS MAKING ME SICK(ER)

Sexism is real.

As a gender-nonconforming, often woman-presenting person living in the US, I know this. I've seen it time and time again, particularly when I was younger.

But sometimes, something happens that really connects the brain to direct experience.

Preamble:

Many years ago, I was in a motorcycle accident. The classic "car made a left turn into me," one block from my San Francisco flat. The car pinned my leg to my bike, knocking me to the ground. Thank the Gods I didn't bash my head. Yeah, I wasn't wearing a helmet.

Because no bones were broken, I was sent home from the hospital with zero treatment, despite the fact that I literally could not walk. After I insisted, they finally consented to give me a cane.

That was round one.

The chronic fatigue symptoms and chronic illness—along with chronic pain that shifted to excruciating pain when my hips slipped further out of alignment—began then. No, I wasn't eligible for physical therapy. No, they wouldn't prescribe chiropractic care or bodywork.

Somehow, I struggled through, despite the fact that it ruined my career as a dancer and therefore I couldn't really pay my bills anymore.

Eventually, when I was working full time in a soup kitchen for room and board, some kind alternative medicine folks helped me, saying that my working for unhoused people was enough trade for their services.

I slowly got better. A bodyworker also figured out how to put my hips back into alignment. The chronic pain eased up.

I did pretty well for a number of years, still getting sick more often than most people, still having trouble maintaining my energy levels consistently, but doing okay by virtue of increasing my exercise regime. Eventually, my punishing travel-for-work schedule did me in, dropping me with burnout and exhaustion despite my great diet, great exercise, great meditation practice.

At that point, I started changing my life, getting ready to eventually leave work that I had loved for many years. I just couldn't do it anymore.

Interregnum, to the Present:

Big life changes slowly made, I'm still tired a lot. Still get a lot of low-grade, annoying illnesses. Still have trouble keeping my energy levels consistent.

I have learned when I can work through it and when I need to actually go back to bed. I've taught myself the difference between "tired" and "exhausted," between "low energy but I can do my work if I just begin" and "in such a brain fog nothing is going to happen, so I'd better either work on something less taxing, or take the afternoon off entirely."

For years, I would say to my (male) doctor: "I'm tired a lot and get sick way more often than I ought to."

For years, he ignored my complaints because I was otherwise healthy. "People can get sick six times a year on average," he would say.

Why I didn't fire him, I'm still not sure. Perhaps because I've never quite trusted Western medicine in the first place, other than for trauma—though they didn't do so well with that after a car slammed into my motorcycle, did they? Perhaps because I otherwise liked him just fine. Perhaps it was laziness, not wanting to vet other doctors, feeling they were all likely the same.

I relied instead on an herbalist and the things I always had relied upon: food, exercise, meditation.

Finally, because of a move to a different state—in an attempt to lower stress levels, for one thing—and with a promise to myself that my health was now my top priority...I noticed that despite lower stress and less intensive responsibilities, I *still* wasn't able to start volunteering like I wanted to. I *still* planned to show up at actions or events and then just didn't make it three quarters of the time.

Because I was too tired. Just like I am, writing this, today.

On my first visit, I told my new doctor I was tired and sick too often. Her response? "Let's run a whole battery of tests."

Finally. A doctor who listened.

Well, I got the results back. My thyroid output is abnormal. It seems that it doesn't produce enough thyroid hormone, so my pituitary gland is always trying to send out signals, trying and failing to convince it to produce more.

My symptoms are pretty classic hypothyroid symptoms. Just as my male doctor not listening to me is a pretty classic sexism symptom.

The new doctor wants me to try some medicine for six weeks and then get my blood levels tested again. I'm hoping that it works, and that this information will also help my herbalist to adjust my formulas better.

But if it turns out hypothyroidism isn't the main culprit? My new doctor is willing to keep trying for other diagnoses until we figure it out.

She actually listened to me, like a doctor is supposed to.

Why Did I Write This Essay?

First of all, because of what I began with: Sexism is real, and has directly affected my health, well-being, and my ability to work.

And we live under interlocking systems that directly increase the deleterious effects of sexism, racism, ableism, ageism...

Second, because as a self-employed author, I'm covered via the ACA—which, imperfect as it is, is now at risk because of entrenched systems of white supremacy, patriarchy, and plutocracy—and I may now end up needing regular medicine, like so many other people do.

And I'm not sure how long my coverage will last. I just hope that my energy and health will be renewed enough for me to do the work I desire, and hope that work will bring in enough to pay for what I need if worse comes to worst.

It's either that, or the toppling of empire and the total rebuilding of society based on compassion rather than punishment.

And I'm still holding out for that, with all my heart.

March, 2017

THIRTY-TWO
BODY. IMAGE.

Recently, poet Jay Hulme shared some anti-trans harassment couched as "concern" that he fielded after posting a sleepy morning photo of himself with his chest bare. You see, the image showed pale white scars. The scars show that he's healed from surgery.

I have those scars, too, though mine are pale pink right now, six months after I went under the knife. Strangely, though, because I didn't have my breasts completely removed, if I showed a photo of myself bare chested here, I'd have to cross out my nipples. Because my body can still be read as a woman's. Even though I'm not, and I never really have been, though when I was younger, I went through phases of trying, mostly out of feminist solidarity.

Now in my early 50s, I have so many stories about my gender non-conformity, and the pushback against it, I don't even know where to begin. What to cut out. What is too much to tell. Too boring. Doesn't fit the narrative.

Just as I've never fit a tidy narrative. I've been queer in so many ways since childhood, since I was asked, repeatedly, whether or not I was a boy or a girl. Since I was too much of everything... Too spiritually fervent. Too intellectual. Too forthright. Too opinionated. Too concerned with injustice. Too...strange. Wanting to kiss girls. Wanting boys to pay attention to me. Wanting to fit in but knowing I never would, so settling instead for standing out.

I've made money exploiting what people think women are, too, as a peep show worker and a dancer. Starting at age thirteen, I've been harassed, threatened, and assaulted for being perceived as "female" and called a dyke and threatened with violence for not being "female" enough. I've had people say they wished I wouldn't write about trans issues, because they read me as cis. I've had people tell me I wasn't butch enough because I didn't bind my breasts. I've had people say I must be femme because I delighted in a rose damask print jacket, only to have me look at them in confusion, because clearly it was the jacket of a dandy.

My gender is the sturdy cadence of boots on concrete, so summers can be hell for more reasons than it is simply hot outside.

I've had people expect me to follow them into the men's room, and yes, I've used the men's room many, many times. I've had people gasp and back out of the women's room when catching the shorn back of my head. I've had trans men recognize that me wearing a dress in ritual was brave, because it was so clearly me, pushing some boundary for the sake of the Gods. I've been quite clear that wearing a corset and tight skirt was me doing drag, and that wearing "regular women's clothing" makes my skin crawl, so I just don't do it. You'll never catch me in a dress.

And my sexuality is as fluid as my gender has always been.

As sexually queer and genderqueer both, I've used the Q word to describe myself for decades, but as language changed—as the definitions of queer shifted, and as insistence on sex and gender binaries came and went and came again—that word became not quite enough to convey my reality to others. But it still conveys my reality to me.

I'm queer as fuck.

I'm a dandy. A peacock. Patterned off of the pop icons of my youth. Grace Jones, my first celebrity crush, who burned me to the core with her power and beauty. Annie Lennox. Boy George. Prince. Suits and makeup. Frills and frock coats. Punks and Goths in eyeliner and black lipstick. Everyone who played with gender because to be beyond gender was to be revealed as who we truly were. Androgynous, it was briefly called. As a teen, I wore men's suits my body swam in, and narrow ties, or 1950s party dresses with leather and chains. As I aged, and my body changed, I wished for crisp shirts and trousers, but my breasts and hips got in the way, so mostly I wore T-shirts and jeans, with fancy jackets over the top of it all.

And I'm impatient with *all* of these images. All these

stories. For one thing, compared to many trans men and trans women—especially BIPOC trans women—I live a life of relative safety and ease, so talking about all of this can sound like so much whining. But also? My stories aren't the *point*. Because frankly, gender itself *has never made sense to me*. So, I've gone along, accepting any and all pronouns, with the people who knew me best seeing me, and the rest of the world? Meh. It would form whatever opinions it wanted. Who has time?

Through all of this, nothing much misgendered me except being called "lady," "miss," or "ma'am," and people using the first name I was given at birth. The only reason I kept that first name—when I legally changed my name decades ago—was to honor the mother who gave it to me.

She's dead now, so I can let it go.

And then one day, my body betrayed me.

I USED to joke that I wished I could donate my hourglass shape to some femme who wanted it. I had to fight to keep correct posture. I had neck and back pain. Eventually, I wore nothing but sports bras to give my breasts extra support, hoping that engineering would take care of the problem. Plus, they minimized my chest—making it a size or two smaller—which was good. But as my body aged, and as I battled a worsening chronic illness and couldn't muster the energy to lift weights to strengthen my back anymore, and as hormonal changes coupled with my illness led to weight gain, my breasts got even larger.

And for the first time I felt gender dysphoria so strongly, so persistently, that I could not bear it anymore. I could not bear to take off my shirt in front of others. I had sex wearing a tank top. All of a sudden, I knew how that felt, that thing some people talked about. And that feeling did not go away.

So finally, I talked with my partners. I checked with my health insurance (thankful to the ACA that allows me, a self-employed person, to afford medical service in this shithole of a country that doesn't believe people deserve even basic care). I asked my former chiropractor if they'd write a letter, attesting to the years of chronic pain. I was thinking about plastic surgery, which terrified me.

When I walked into the surgeon's office that first time, just checking in with the receptionist almost caused me to burst into tears. I managed to keep it together during my meeting with the surgeon. Not once did I talk about my dysphoria, because I knew that would complicate things, elongating the process. I wasn't choosing full top surgery, though I considered it. I just wanted my breasts much, much, smaller. More in keeping with this in-between being that I am.

I was so emotional after that appointment I had to ask a partner to please meet me for lunch because I couldn't make it home, and I also couldn't bear to be alone with all the inchoate feelings. It was overwhelming, the sense that I could possibly become more of who I already had been all of these years. That my body might, just might, reflect my inner landscape more closely than it had before. But even these words are not correct, they are just my mind, all these months later, trying to make sense of a visceral, animal sense that something momentous was about to occur. And that something had to do with body. With image. And with how the society I live in assigns and telegraphs gender.

I waited until January to have the surgery, wanting to use the dark of winter as an excuse to slow down, to lie in bed and recover. My chronic illness got so bad that there was some concern I should not got through with the operation. But once decided, there was no way I was going to put it off.

Five hours of surgery later, with the surgeon having removed just under three pounds from my chest, I came to, shivering violently, moaning, with nurses piling warmed blankets on top of me. I heard my partner's voices before being yanked back under the dark waters.

In the weeks that followed, I dealt with nausea, and being unable to lift anything heavier than my travel kettle. I walked around with T-rex arms so I wouldn't reach for anything, until my lymphatic system started to rebel from lack of movement. My partners were awesome, doing for me what I could not do until I was sick of it. I dealt with shooting pain as nerves regrew, with hard, subcutaneous scarring that I was assured would soften over time.

But when I went for a walk, the good posture I'd struggled with came naturally for the first time in memory.

And as my breasts healed—still slightly larger than I

requested, because breast reduction is an inexact science, but at least half of their original size—I felt at ease in my body for the first time in years. This was the body I was meant to have. This was what it felt like to feel free. The swagger I'd been missing? It came back. It felt as if I always had my gender-correct boots on, even in house slippers.

Two months ago, one of my partners took me to celebrate. We went to Nordstrom Rack where I bought two of the dandiest dandy blazers in the men's department, and they fit. They finally hung properly on my frame. Oh, I'm rolling up the sleeves until I can take them to a tailor, but here I am, a non-binary they, with a body that more closely reflects what's always been inside.

And then, more recently, a friend who works for a lawyer's office asked if I wanted help with a name and gender marker change. Because having to travel under the first name of a person I haven't been in twenty-five years grates. And having receptionists call that name out and needing to answer to it until I can correct them, grates.

I said yes. I am now legally who I've always been inside.

I'm still the Thorn I've been for decades, even before I changed my name, but my first initial T is now a magical working that I hope will amuse me each time an airline employee or receptionist uses it. I'll tell it to you here, as long as you promise to call me Thorn: my first name is now Thankful.

And my new gender?

It's a jaunty X.

. . .

Portland, OR
September, 2019

2025 AUTHOR'S NOTE:

Since writing this essay, things have grown exponentially worse for trans and queer people in the US. My state ID has reflected my correct name and gender marker since 2019. That felt like enough, since I have not traveled outside the US in years.

However, in late 2024, once the new administration was confirmed, I ordered an expedited passport and passport card with my correct gender marker. The passport arrived, but the card never did and never will. The US Federal Government is no longer changing gender markers. This means a schlep to the DMV to get a Real ID—and hope that works because the state of Oregon still honors gender marker changes— and possibly a call to California to change the marker on my birth certificate. Why? Because the current information being spread states that all documents must match. And who knows when they'll start asking white people for our papers. They're already asking people with brown skin.

My marriage may end up null and void in the future, as well, as may the marriages of some of my friends.

But we're not giving up. And we are not complying in advance.

2019 Author's Note:

I want to thank the Millennial and Gen Z gender outlaws for pushing through recent, more binary cultural language phases and insisting on the term "non-binary." I'd still rather have no gender at all, but as long as I'm forced into it, non-binary is as good a term as any. Thanks, too, for the insistence that—like "man" or "woman"—non-binary does not have to look any particular way.

I wrote this for anyone who needs it. Thanks for listening.

THIRTY-THREE
FOR NEX BENEDICT, IN LOVE AND RAGE

The children were trained by adults. Trained toward hatred. Trained toward violence. Their fists struck, powered by the voices of their parents, their teachers, and the hatred spewing from their phones.

It was expected, wasn't it? To gang up against the different one? The one who dressed like a budding dandy, who called themselves Nex, and whose friends knew them as he or they, him or them. Especially when Nex had the temerity to defend himself.

No ambulance was called by the school.

Nex died for no reason other than this: some adults cannot allow anyone who looks, or acts, or feels differently than they do to live.

The state school superintendent of Oklahoma—Ryan Walters—pushes anti-LGBTQ+ policies. He appointed Chaya Raichik—who does not live in Oklahoma—to an advisory council that oversees the state school libraries. Children are not allowed to change their gender on school records. Owasso High School insists that students use the bathroom of the gender they were assigned at birth.

This scenario is not just happening in Oklahoma. It is happening all over the country. Families are fleeing places, from the Southern states through the Northeast... fearing for their children's lives. But with 463 proposed anti-LGBTQ+ laws and bills throughout the country, there are scant places left to go.

If you are an adult, and not doing your best right now to help the children in your lives? The different ones. The strange ones. The ones who don't quite fit the status quo?

You are remiss in your duties.

If you are a parent who cannot find a way to love your own child? I have no words for you. You are not worth my breath.

I've written and written and written about queer joy and queer rage. I've written about racial and economic justice. About disability and courage. Those words I wield so cleverly sometimes?

They did not save Nex. To the teens who wielded their parent's words, pummeling him to the floor? Nex was just another strange, Indigenous teen who dared to be himself. Nex became—to them—a thing to be bullied, not a person to be cherished. A person to be saved.

The United States is a dangerous place for trans people right now. It is a frightening place for queer people right now. It always has been, but yes, in this moment, it is also worse. I've lived through the decades of gay bashing and the AIDS epidemic, of Matthew Shepherd and too many Black trans women killed to count.

And right now? Some very warped and angry, smug, and powerful people are poised against us. Sowing hatred. Promulgating fear. Scaremongering. Engaging in acts of stochastic terrorism that leave too many dead.

Think the Libs of TikTok aren't coming for you, too? They are. The laws to control bodily autonomy are everywhere. Women are still dying. Birth centers closing. Bathrooms policed. Too many are locked in prisons for no crime other than being poor.

The billionaires don't care about us.

The politicians don't care about us.

The shareholders don't care about us.

They don't care about the multiple genocides happening, other than finding the ways they can profit. And they cannot profit from queer or trans children. Not enough.

They manipulate us into thinking that someone else is the real problem, the real danger, the real threat. Someone like Nex, who tried to defend himself, and whose soft body fell to the bathroom floor. Someone like a parent at the southern border, worried that their kids won't make it through the night.

All we have is each other. What are you doing about it? How will you choose to help?

March, 2024

THIRTY-FOUR
OUR QUEER LOVE WILL NOT DIE

"It's still a world with plums in it, my loves, and chamomile, lipstick, and cellos. It's still a world with us in it. Find a hand and hold on."

— Elena Rose

PICTURE THIS: a wedding photo taken in a garden, with trees behind. Two middle-aged, nonbinary, bi/pan white people clasp each other, heads tucked close, joy shining on their faces.

That's me, the short one in the navy and white polka-dot men's blazer with my glasses and super-short hair, and my partner, the tall one in a dress, wearing the gorgeous makeup, hair curling softly past their chin. We have both been queer and gender fluid since childhood, but, being middle-aged now, there was not always the language to describe us growing up.

Sometimes we took questioning or abuse, sometimes we tried to hide. I was never very successful at the latter, being too strange in too many different ways.

We found each other nineteen years ago, and formed a strange, queer family with other people along the way. We formed household with friends, family, and my other —platonic—partner, whose romantic partner lives nearby.

This household has shifted and changed over the years, with people coming and going. Our family, though? That keeps expanding ever outward, whether the people live with us or not.

Because when you're queer, you make family from the people you find along the way. When you're queer, family looks and feels like what you make it.

The two of us have supported each other through good and rough times. We married on our seventeenth anniversary in a small, ten-minute ceremony in our back-yard, during a bad phase of the pandemic, with around a dozen local friends in attendance. That's where the photo I describe above was taken.

And we're surviving in the midst of the rise of fascism and intolerance yet again. We're surviving in the midst of the murders of trans women, and gay bashings, and club shootings, and bans, and restrictions, and hate.

You'd better believe we have an agenda.

Our queer agenda is: More love. More life. More joy.

Queer love looks like doing the dishes.

Queer love looks like puttering in the garden.

Queer love looks like eating cashew ice cream.

Queer love looks like reading books or watching movies.

Queer love looks like waiting in the emergency room.

Queer love looks like building a fire in winter.

Queer love looks like a child seeing themselves reflected in the world around them, and deciding they are beautiful.

Unfortunately, our queer agenda also includes rage.

Because...

Queer life is wondering whether your partner is safe if they go out en femme.

Queer life wonders which public restroom you're going to get called out for using.

Queer life is the person at the Social Security office apologizing for not having a non-binary gender marker box to check.

Queer life is being threatened with violence because you don't look the way a bigot thinks you should.

Queer life is standing outside a school with trans and rainbow flags because their optional, student-led Pride celebration was canceled because of death threats by right wing bullies.

Queer life is knowing that your loved ones are in danger and that this danger is supported by some of the people who are supposed to love you, but who don't, really. Because you refuse to change who you are, and for some reason, they can't love that at all.

To be queer is to feel angry and heartbroken at the way your friends are treated, and at the fact that too many of them are now dead.

To be queer is to say "fuck you" to the bigots, and the haters, and those who want you to simply disappear.

To be queer is to shine in our joy, and to know, even though posting a photo of love on the Internet might cause disgusting backlash...that it is important, because, to paraphrase Harvey Milk, we have to give young people —in Missouri, Florida, Arizona, Alabama, and Texas—hope.

We have to say, *"Hey! We've both known we were genderqueer since around age six. We've both known we weren't straight since around age twelve. We survived. We created family. We are living our lives."*

We're here. We're queer. We're in love.

You bigots? Search your hearts and find some compassion instead of self-righteous arrogance. And if you can't do that? Leave us the fuck alone.

You supporters? Agitate the systems of power that wish to crush your family and friends. Call out bigotry. Offer time or money or space to people needing to flee unsafe situations. Provide a haven when and where you can.

You queer people? Find a friend. Whisper your secrets in the dark. Plant a flower. Dance in your bedroom. Dance in the streets. Shout when you need to. Smash if you need to. Then fall in love with yourself and with this earth.

We are all we have, and we can hold each other, because as James Baldwin said:

"The sea rises, the light fails, lovers cling to each other, and children cling to us. The moment we cease to hold

each other, the moment we break faith with one another, the sea engulfs us and the light goes out."

Let us be light for each other. Let us find one another like stars shining in the velvet night.

They can kill us, but our queer love will not die.

We are eternal.

T. Thorn Coyle
June 2023

PART 6
THE LONG HAUL

THIRTY-FIVE

INVOKE PURPOSE, NOT DESPAIR

ON LIFE IN (CRUMBLING) EMPIRE

Don't give up.

Don't freak out.

Freaking out helps no one. Following every single atrocity helps no one. Stuffing your heart, mind, and soul with pain helps no one.

Be aware of the suffering. Be aware of the stakes. Then move away from the terror for a moment. Breathe. Center. Pray if that's what you do. Breathe again. Take a drink of water (I hope your water is clean). Eat something (I hope you have access to nourishment). Sleep if need be (I hope you have a safe place to rest).

Don't give up.

Don't freak out. Or if you are freaking out, do your best to ask for help with it. Do your best to access your coping mechanisms. What comforts you? Seek it out.

THERE IS TOO MUCH GOING on for any one person to process. Fires. Wars. Starvation. Die offs. Mass migrations. Deaths. Mass Imprisonment. Rape. Fascism. Hatred. Children in cages. Images of animals in burning landscapes.

TAKE A BREATH. Find your center. Take another breath.

Slow your breathing down. Way down. Try to inhale and exhale evenly.

Do what you need to to take care of yourself. Ask for help if you need it.

Then organize. Find a group already doing work. Plug in. Or gather your family and friends.

Do one thing to help. One thing. Do one more if you have the time, energy, or money.

Connect: with community, with purpose, with your center, with what helps.

WE NEED PURPOSE NOW, not despair.

We need anger, and focus, and love.

We need the consistent showing up in as many ways as possible, to the possibility of justice.

We need to keep envisioning a world that cares, and build that world, together, in our own small ways.

No one is off the hook from this. Every human has to try. Those of us barely making it right now? The place you start is by asking for help. Or by just getting yourself through the day.

Those of us who have more breathing room? Stop spiraling into the long scrolling litany of rage and despair.

Find a place to anchor. Then do something. Do any blessed thing you can.

Feed someone.

Clothe someone.

Make phone calls.

Teach something restorative.

Donate to smaller organizations doing on the ground work (Pro tip: do not donate to massive operations that help no one but the CEO).

Listen to those most directly impacted. Follow their lead when possible.

Protest.

Blockade.

Do banner drops.

Keep the pressure on those who hold political and institutional power.

Write to corporation heads, demanding they change.

If you have money? Give it away.

Directly confront racism, misogyny, fascism, and other forms of hate and oppression.

There are thousands of ways to help....

GET ANGRY, but don't stew about it. Act.

Disrupt acts of oppression (Practice how you might do that with your friends).

Sabotage the machines of oppression.

Live your life the best you absolutely can.

And the more comfort you live with? (Clean water. A safe bed. Decent food. Family not incarcerated. Health care.) The more we're counting on you to listen to those who don't have these things, and to act in ways that help.

As long as we have each other, hope is never lost.

TL;DR: Keep breathing. Don't give up. Ask for help if you need it. Organize. Plug in. Drink some water. Do one thing. Then another.

January, 2020

THIRTY-SIX

WAKING UP WORRIED

THE DAY AFTER THE INAUGURATION

As Inauguration Day 2021 wore on, my brief flash of joy that Trump was gone slowly descended into feeling not right. I slept for ten hours—a feat for me—and woke up uneasy. Worried. Even as people celebrated in the streets, that worry would not leave me. So I wrote:

THERE IS no ebullience in my heart today. No sense of relief. Instead, pressure pushes at my chest. It takes concentration to sink back into meditation. To follow my breath. Listen to the whir of the furnace kicking on. Watch the flickering candle flame.

The pressure on my chest is a deep sense of worry.

The trauma isn't over. The healing has nowhere near begun.

Perhaps this is a vestige of my childhood trauma, reaching up to grip my heart with its tiny, fragile, fist. That fist knows the tyrant is never really gone. Perhaps he is sleeping. Or drunk in a bar. Or off building houses. That tiny fist knows that violence is random, quick, irrational, and never far away.

There is always another shoe, waiting to drop.

Yes, perhaps that is some part of this.

BUT THAT IS NOT ALL this worry is.

I've worried for months, of course, about what will happen when people's unemployment runs out, or when the eviction moratoriums cease. I've shouted at politicians since March about rent and mortgage freezes and forgiveness, not this deferral of future disaster.

But at least for the past six months or so, I knew that as many of us as possible were pulling together to make sure people were taken care of if it was at all within our power. We shared resources. Gathered food and delivered water. Checked on neighbors. Taught children. Showed up for Black and Indigenous communities...

I did not have to worry that all the people who only woke up to realize there was a problem in our country back in 2018 would fall back into complacent sleep.

But I'm worried about that now.

Worried that the status quo will return to its oppressive, crushing equilibrium inside us, and be an unshakeable force once more.

We must still shake the tree, my friends. We must still share what resources we have. We must still rage in the streets. We must still hold fast to one another and make sure that we don't starve, or founder in exhaustion, or drown.

Love does not sleep, my friends. Love keeps watch on what it loves.

Love also keeps watch on the enemies of love.

NOW THAT THE proximate threat has flown off in a helicopter, do we even see the danger anymore?

There is no "wait and see."

There is no "give it time."

Too many are dead. Too many mourn. Too many live on the knife's edge of precarity.

White supremacists still threaten people's homes with fires and people's heads with bats. They still threaten immigrants and activists and anyone they perceive as not exactly like them.

The day after inauguration, after waking up with the worried pressure in my chest, I saw the news from my local streets. A cop pulled a knife on a protestor. Neo-nazis called a reporter "jihadi." That same reporter was later sent to the hospital outside of the ICE facility because BORTAC and DHS set off a flash bang near her ear and filled a candlelight vigil with clouds of CS gas without warning. They arrested indigenous women with flowers, and a white man in a wheelchair.

The NYPD are still tackling people to the ground. Our prisons and jails are filled with Covid and lock downs and suffering. The carceral state is still the only weapon our country seems to use as a tool of justice. There are still drones to drop bombs.

The bulk of our resources still go to punishment and war.

There are children in cages.

We still seek to punish, when what we must seek is accountability.

And across the country, people still don't have clean water.

And across the country, people still sleep on icy sidewalks.

And across the country, billionaires hoard wealth and resources as their workers die.

The abusive tyrant has not gone away, because the abusive tyrant is a great dragon snaking its way through every level of our society. It whispers in our ears that it will keep us safe as it drips poison into the water from its venomous fangs.

DIG IN YOUR HEELS. Hold out a hand. Find a way to love. Find an action that speaks that love to the world. There are thousands of small connections to be made. Millions. We are all cells in the same body. We can help one another survive, and even thrive.

We need accountability from all of those who hold the knife—and they are legion.

And we need to continue to do our best to help each other through. To fashion a new society that is better than the old.

We need to dream better, wilder, dreams.

We need to breathe.

I'm with you, my friends. I hope that you are with me, too.

Don't Give Up.

January, 2021

THIRTY-SEVEN
DISRUPTING OPPRESSION

A short list of other possible disruptions of the culture of oppression:

- If transit police, ICE, CBP, or police are harassing someone, assess the situation.
- Is it safe for you to speak up? (The feeling of safety is different for all of us, depending on our personal situation. If what we are feeling is *uncomfortable* rather than actually *unsafe*, it is up to us to push ourselves to speak and act).
- Are there others around that you can enlist to help intervene?
- Film. Take photos. Record names or badge numbers if possible. If you are willing and able, follow police/immigration if they try to take someone away.
- If the person being harassed or taken wants

to, get their name and if possible, a contact phone number.

- Disrupt racist, misogynist, homophobic, trans antagonist etc comments and jokes.
- Explain why they are hurtful and bigoted.
- If someone is in possible danger, assess the situation.
- Are there others around to help?
- In what way are you willing and able to intervene? With your voice? By calling for help? With your body?
- Sometimes even letting the aggressor know you are witnessing is enough.
- Offer to walk a harassed person to a safer place, or if you have the funds, call a Lyft for them.
- Offer direct support to grassroots groups run by affected communities. Time. Money. Amplification of the cause.
- Offer direct support to unhoused neighbors. Ask for what they want or need.
- Call your local government to protest the treatment of unhoused neighbors, the poor, immigrants, or others.
- Attend City Council meetings and agitate for better mental health care and fewer arrests.
- Tell businesses who harass vulnerable or oppressed people that you will not spend money with them.
- Share pertinent, timely, helpful information

in your social networks (inflammatory articles and memes are most often not helpful).

- Seek out education on issues and cultures you know little to nothing about.
- Write, sing, dance, make art that contributes to the world you want to see.
- Grow food and give it away.

2021

THIRTY-EIGHT
POUR WATER FOR THE THIRSTY

Sometimes we worry because we want to control the outcome.

Sometimes we worry because we care, yet feel helpless to act.

In the Tarot deck illustrated by Pamela Coleman Smith, the Five of Cups shows a person standing over three spilled cups, head hanging low. Behind the person are two other cups, filled to the brim and ready to offer sustenance. Yet, these two cups are ignored. The person focuses on what has been lost, and worries that fulfillment, comfort, or nourishment will never come again.

AS I WRITE THIS, the world around us can feel out of control on a daily basis. Covid still kills. India and Pakistan have reached record and untenable temperatures. The ice caps melt. Human rights are violated daily.

Black trans women are murdered. Indigenous women are missing. War ravages Ukraine, Palestine, Yemen, and too many other places. In the US, abortion is on the chopping block, as are trans and gay rights. Prisons are filled to bursting. There is little justice to be found anywhere, it seems.

These problems are too large for one person to face alone. So, we worry. We rage. We avoid. We drink. We feel defeated. We crawl back into bed. We pound the pavement and hold signs. We break windows. We cry.

It becomes harder and harder to not focus on what is broken and despair.

I COMPREHEND this sense of anger and defeat. Like many of you, I've worked most of my life to shift despair into hope and to channel the anger into action. I've done so since age thirteen when I first became concerned about the twin issues of environmental devastation and the death penalty. Others have fought longer and harder than I have and organized with greater success.

I bless those organizers every day.

And not all of us are cut out for that. Not everyone is Ai-Jen Poo or Lucy Parsons, Chris Smalls or Fannie Lou Hamer, Pinar Sinopoulos-Lloyd, Mariame Kaba, or Sophie Scholl. But you know what? At rock bottom, all of these people know—or knew—there is no way to do what is necessary alone. Every organizer needs people like you and me. People to speak up. People to show up. People to help gather supplies. Roll bandages. Make connections.

Pass out info. Plant food. Care for children. Stock pantries. Share resources and skills. Find other ways to live.

Every organizer needs people to say, "I am here. How can I help?"

THE OLIGARCHS and plutocrats and mutual political backscratchers have destroyed so much. They've smashed large and beautiful things into smaller and smaller pieces.

It is up to us to care for those small pieces to the best of our abilities. I'll repeat my old refrain: *Do what you can, when you can, where you can.*

How do we start? Look at your skills, interests, resources, connections, and energy levels. Then find one simple way to be of service. Find a way to show you care. Find a way to show up for this bleeding, beautiful society on this gasping planet.

And remember to breathe. Remember there are flowers and trees and music and books.

In the midst of that which is broken, things grow and become whole. In the midst of hardship, life takes root.

WE ARE ALL WE HAVE, my friends. Each other, the sun, this earth, these oceans, and this sky. We are not empty cups, spilled out and broken. We still have life-giving water to pour out for one another.

Do not despair, or not for long. Hold out a hand to offer what you have. And don't forget to dance.

May 2022

THIRTY-NINE
METAL FATIGUE
ON THE USE OF LOVE IN TIMES OF STRESS

Blessed be these times. Blessed be our communities. Blessed be the strength in our hearts. Blessed be the power of love.

Don't let the alt-right/misogynists/fascists/racists/plutocrats/ableists/transphobes/queer bashers/white-supremacists/anti-Muslims/anti-Semites/anti-immigrants/jerks/bullies/shamers/oppressors grind you down.

Don't let the world itself stress and bend you until you finally break.

Seriously. Don't let it happen.

Metal fatigue.*

The process of constant stress and pressure applied repeatedly in cycles until an object finally cracks and breaks.

Metal fatigue.

It's happening. To bodies, minds, and souls.

Right now.

Every time you open social media. Or glance at the news. Or for some of you, every time you go to a restaurant, or shop, or a park, or go to work.

There it is! Another terrible thing happening! Another thing attacking you! Another thing you aren't sure what exactly, if anything, you can do about. Another thing you are weary of countering.

And another!

And another!

Rend! Rip! Bend!

Hundreds of tiny injuries are inflicted on your psyche. Repeatedly.

Tiny tugs. Tiny bits of pressure. Here. Then there. Then here again.

These seem inconsequential at first, until your whole being is bowed and bloody with them.**

You begin to collapse from the weakening of your life force. The leeching away of your power.

You crack.

You crumble into yourself.

Sometimes you look for distraction in the usual ways...only to find that there is little distraction to be had.

This stuff is everywhere you look. Always creating more fissures in your heart.

Fatigue failure happens over time, because of repeated stress cycles. Fatigue failure occurs even when an object has not reached its strength limits.

Fatigue failure is caused by consistent stress and pressures that wear an object down.

So what do you do? How do you interrupt a stress cycle? And how do you build in resilience before the stress cycles begin?

One way is to consistently invoke love.

The love that feels like bedrock.

Or the love that feels like interstitial flow.

The love that takes your breath away, and fills your eyes with tears of gratitude.

The love that gives your life back.

Not romance. Not heartbreak. Not selfishness. Not co-dependency. Not limerence. Not...any of the forms love can be shaped into. Invoke the original force.

Love. Connection. Empowerment. Ease. And perhaps a dash of revitalizing lust.

When hundreds of tiny assaults are bending and pressing and bleeding you dry, take a breath. Feel the pain. Tense all the way up with it. Then exhale. And let it go.

Then ask yourself: How can I best invoke love right now?

Then ask: What feels closest to my heart, or most aligned with my abilities?

Focus on that love.

Then do that thing.

Don't wallow in the awareness of all the things you cannot save.

Don't continuously batter yourself from the inside with the things that strike at you from the outside.

Offer the help you can.

Receive the help you can.

Offer the help you can.

Receive the help you can.

Offer the help you can.

Invoke more love.

Every day.

The slices and assaults will still come. But the next time? You'll be able to say: "I feel you. And today, I'm doing this thing to help build or preserve or protect the things that feel important to me, and I'm calling on love to help me."

Then remind your friends:

They love something, too.

Love builds. Love repairs. Love is strong.

And a bunch of tiny invocations can increase the strength of love. Art. Music. Laughter. Food. Sharing. Mutual aid.

Supporting acts of love counters our fatigue.

Embracing acts of love increases our endurance.

Help shore up the things that matter to you most, and help your friends and community do the same.

We build from there.

Stay in love. Always. Or for as long as you can.

DECEMBER, 2016

Other practical suggestions in no particular order:

- Unplug from phones and computers for set periods of time.
- If possible, set computers/phones to red tones instead of blue.***

- Get out in trees, or water, or desert, or rain... anyplace outside if you can.
- Talk with friends and loved ones.
- Pay your bills.
- Eat nourishing food.
- Listen to music, look at art.
- Remember to ask for help.

December, 2016

Footnotes:

*Thanks to a scientist friend who reminded me of this term when I was casting about for a good descriptor not based on racist idioms (the kernel of this essay began with "death by a thousand cuts," which has racist roots).

**For those who don't experience it, this is similar to what many marginalized people experience consistently with what are called "micro-aggressions." The tiny insults, slights, and actions that...add up over time, until the person is made sick by them.

***This suggestion comes from a friend trained in Traditional Chinese Medicine

FORTY
REFILL THE WELL

Every day it's one more thing. Sometimes several things at a time.

Fire.

Flooding.

Death.

Disease.

Poverty.

Injustice.

Corruption.

Shootings.

Bombs.

Another Black or Native person killed.

Another cop goes free.

And here we are, trying to live.

It can feel overwhelming.

POOR, oppressed, and marginalized people know that

one must rest when one can, and take joy when one can, because tomorrow may bring more hardship and pain.

Meanwhile, we are too little connected.

We are too much connected.

We are connected in ways that all too often do not include the touch of voice or hands, or a clear way forward.

So what do we do? As always, we find ways to reach out and do what we can. We find ways to show up, to offer, to listen, to ask.

THE OTHER THING we can do is to remember to refill the well.

Drink in the scent of pine or amber sweat.

Drink in the taste of water on our lips.

Drink in laughter.

Drink in poetry.

Drink in music. Dancing. Squirrels and pigeons. Crows and love. Datura and bougainvillea and roses and mesas and mountains and oceans and street art and apples and children and books and sun and wind.

Don't give up. Life isn't only a state of emergency.

THIS WORK we're all engaged in with one another? It's a long haul. It always has been.

Take a moment. Breathe. Refill your well. Then find a way to pour.

FORTY-ONE
THE LONG HAUL
CREATIVITY, COMMUNITY, AND LIFE

Writer Kristine Kathryn Rusch wrote a recent blog about the need for creative people to give ourselves some space right now.

Breathing room is important. I've been watching people around me struggle. I've been watching violence erupting in the streets as anti-vaxxers and white supremacists rally, prepared for violence against anyone who disagrees. I've been watching people facing eviction. Hurricanes smashing city infrastructures. Floods. Fires. Wars. Mass displacement. Rising temperatures and water levels. Melting ice, dead salmon, shrinking habitats. Billionaires getting richer. Orange skies.

The toll is huge, in pain, loss, and in the emotional and psychic burden caused by simply caring about it all.

For some of us, it makes it hard to sleep.

For others, it makes it hard to get out of bed.

Others of us slow down or crash from anger or despair.

Some of us bury ourselves in work, hoping the problems will go away if we do something—anything—else hard enough.

Doom scrolling. Volunteering. Mutual aid. Raising funds. Helping friends and family. All of this activity is happening right now as we scramble to figure out the shape of the world as it is.

And yeah, there is still fruit on the trees, flowers blooming, fledglings molting. There is still water to carry, and smiles to be had.

I'm grateful. Even in the midst of the pain.

And I'm once again reassessing, and cultivating ways to slow down inside.

COVID-19 and its variants and the consequences of the bungled response from governments and all the rest? Not going away.

Refugees? Not going away.

Climate disaster—which many of us have been shouting warnings about for decades? Not going away.

Greed and the consequently brutal poverty? Not going away.

We are living in the new normal, and we need to figure out how we can adjust to treating this as the long haul.

AS AN INDIVIDUAL, I recently did a major reassessment, with the attitude that all this is not a temporary blip. These rolling crises are just the way life is.

This enabled me to add up my projected work projects, my health vagaries, the stress of current life, my physical, emotional, and spiritual needs, and the needs of folks around me, and folks experiencing crisis further away.

Then I reworked my business plan. I now have a flexible, adjustable plan that keeps me moving toward concrete goals, while including plenty of breathing room. Plenty of space to go for walks. To take photographs. To read. To watch a movie. To have the occasional outdoor dinner or writing date with friends.

I've always been ambitious, but ambition cannot rule out the need to plan for hardship. If we are always working full tilt toward our goals? Not only do we miss out on life and learning and beautiful moments, we also have no capacity to deal with crisis, short or long term.

So I've tailored my ambitions to a less stressful pace. That adjustment meant that just this week, I was able to add something to my plate. A project that will both help me learn some things about my craft, and meet some ancillary goals.

Didn't that add stress? No. It has done the opposite. Flexibility, remember? Long term goals. By adding this project, I'm internally taking stress off all my other projects. Putting them into perspective. Making them not "important."

Creating stories, running a publishing company, and connecting with my community? They're just things that

I do, like prayer and meditation, my daily walks, drinking tea, and talking with neighborhood cats.

I'm in this for the long haul, inside this new normal in what could be a pretty terrifying world.

JUST AS I reassessed my personal business plan, we can do this as communities.

Look around. Who is actually helping people, on the ground? Can you find ways to support them?

Look around. Are there people at work you can organize with?

Is there a free pantry in your neighborhood that needs regular stocking? Does your neighborhood need a free pantry?

Do friends need childcare?

Are there immigrants who need help navigating local systems? Children who need tutoring? Elders who need wood chopped or medicines delivered? Are there pipelines to stop? Oil companies to disrupt? Trans or queer youth who need support? Unhoused people who need back up, or clothing washed, or support interfacing with City Hall? Generic Plan B to be purchased, stockpiled, or gotten to groups helping folks in anti-abortion states?

As infrastructure crumbles and is washed or burned away, setting up systems of community mutual aid is necessary for this long haul. For as many of us to survive and have a chance to strive, we must help one another.

Take stock. What resources, skills, or talents do you have to share? What resources, skills, or talents do other community members have? How can you network with each other so resources and skills are shared, rather than hoarded or gone unused?

What do your neighbors need?

What do you have to offer?

SLOW DOWN. Take a deep breath in. Pause a moment. Then exhale, slowly.

If the world we live in now is indeed the new normal, how can you adjust?

How *will* you adjust?

What personal choices and plans must you reassess?

What community efforts are possible?

Where do you fit in?

We all have a beautiful life to live, right now.

We all have plans, goals, and things to offer. We all need rest, and beauty, and time.

What is one way you can offer yourself more space?

What is one way you can lower your stress levels, and allow body, heart, mind, and soul to breathe a bit more easily?

What can you gift yourself, today, that will support your longevity and resilience? Did you drink some water? Take your meds? Talk with a friend? Get some sleep? Exercise? Escape into a book, movie, or music for a bit? Experience nature?

And what can you offer the world? If not today, then this week. If not this week, this month.

Don't know the answers to some of these questions?

I encourage you to take the time to ponder, brainstorm, write things down. Then talk to your friends and neighbors.

If we're in this—together—for the long haul, we need a plan.

September, 2021

FORTY-TWO

TO BE MORE EFFECTIVE

WE MUST SLOW DOWN INSIDE

This week, I got the message, "Slow down." It came in the form of a rune. Isa. Ice. One straight line carved into a smooth piece of wood. Another interpretation, at least this week, could be, "Chill out."

It's no surprise that I pulled that rune during a week filled with work-related stress, an existential crisis about the state of the world, and with day after day filled with the news of human suffering.

But really, "Chill out?"

How can we chill out or slow down when there is work to be done, and tasks to finish, and personal problems to figure out?

How can we chill out or slow down when there are genocides occurring, and autistic Black kids getting killed while holding gardening tools, and another trans teen bullied to death?

How can we chill out or slow down when the planet is in pain?

The answer is: we must.

Years ago, I studied the Gurdjieff Work. One lesson that Gurdjieff taught his students was to work quickly and quietly at a task like doing the dishes. Have you ever tried to quickly clean a sink filled with dishes while remaining quiet? It is difficult. To accomplish doing something both quickly and quietly requires paying attention...and slowing down inside.

To slow down inside, I've realized over the years, is to be present in the moment while having a well-regulated central nervous system. When we speed up inside, we become agitated, clumsy, less precise, overwhelmed. Our central nervous system goes into overdrive, causing a cascade of physiological and psychological ramifications. Our heart rate spikes. Our breathing constricts. Our digestion rebels. We have trouble sleeping, or perhaps we want to do nothing but sleep. Our brains have trouble coping.

When we speed up inside—not from a burst of joy or excitement, but from stress or anxiety—we become less effective in how we respond to the world. We react instead of choosing.

Right now? We need to slow down *because* we need to choose.

We need to ask: What is important? What is *actually* important? Not simply what is the biggest source of stress in the moment.

When we pause—to take some deep breaths, to re-center ourselves, to go for a walk, or sit in prayer or meditation, or rest beneath a weighted blanket—choice opens once again. We realize we have options. And if we are currently fortunate enough to not be living in an active battleground, I hope we honor those options.

By choosing to not live as if we are in an active battleground when we are not, we can offer help more effectively.

Is there a family who needs us? Can we feed someone? Can we write, or call, or join with friends in a targeted blockade? Can we listen to a teen who's having trouble? Can we speak up? Can we listen more closely? Can we send money to someone who is offering direct help to those in need?

What is the next thing on our plate that needs to be addressed? Is that work problem really life or death? Likely not.

And what is one thing we can do to help the world? What is one thing we can do to alleviate suffering, right now?

It takes each of us doing that one thing, collectively. We hold each other, as James Baldwin once said, because the moment we stop, "the sea engulfs us, and the light goes out."

We hold each other, and we breathe. We invoke hope, and then take action to build a kinder world to come.

So today, I'm slowing down enough to choose.

How about you?

March, 2024

PART 7
ON JOY AND MUTUAL AID

FORTY-THREE
STOKING THE CREATIVE FIRES
IN A WORLD OF DOOM

"Daily new reminders of the forces we have been pushing against in the march toward positive change. It feels so fragile. Baby steps so hard."

– Tananarive Due

Baby steps are hard. But they are deeply important to take.

A friend asked recently if I was feeling extra anxiety lately. My reply?

"I'm feeling more determined."

That determination is what drives me to the gym. It drives me to study. It drives me to write. It drives me to pray. It drives me to speak out. It drives me to show up.

I have determined that building culture is important.

I am determined that these greedy, short-sighted, violent, bigoted fools shall not win.

Right after the 2016 election results rolled in, many artists wrote about how to get through these times.

Well, we need to keep figuring that out, don't we?

And the truth is? People always have.

People figured out how to create during the worst years of the AIDS crisis when queer artists, agitators, and friends were sacrificed on the altar of indifference and fear and a whole generation of queer mentors was decimated.

People figured out how to create when the CIA flooded US city streets with cocaine traded for arms to crush communities in Nicaragua.

People figured out how to create when the wealthy few worked their family members half to death.

People figured out how to create as their cities burned.

People figured out how to create when their communities were bombed.

Some people have always figured out how to create in brutally worse conditions than many of us can imagine.

To create in the face of such opposition is, in itself, a victory.

I don't care if your work is "any good."

I don't care if your work feels "important."

What I care is that everyone who wants to create right now finds a way to say "fuck you" to oppression, depression, despair, illness, poverty, death threats, harassment, betrayal, silence, oblivion, and anything else stacked up against them.

And I know that's hard.

And I know I'm speaking from relative privilege right now.

And I know we can't all feel determined every single day.

We need each other. We need one other person to tag team or relay with. We need one other person who cares.

And we need to listen to that person: whether we share the same physical space, or they are part of a network two continents away.

Please, I beg of you: take a breath right now. Drop your attention deep into your body. Exhale. Then dig deep and find whatever determination rests within you. Breathe into your determination. Increase its power.

Then, ask what will support that determination.

Is it listening to or making music?

Is it reading or writing?

Is it dancing?

Is it digging your fingers into soil?

Is it deep conversations with friends?

Is it laughter?

Is it making sure you eat?

Is it doing your laundry?

Is it going for a walk?

Is it letting yourself feel angry, sorrowful, alienated, or afraid?

Is it choosing to put time on your calendar to create?

Times of Doom always cycle. For millennia, they have risen and fallen like the tides. They are always felt more acutely by oppressed and marginalized people.

If oppressed people stopped creating, even in the face

of death, we would all be lesser for it. We would be missing whole swathes of creative culture.

I don't blame you for wanting to give up.

I just hope and pray you don't.

We are in a time of Doom.

We are also in a time of Possibility.

Please. Find your will. Hold fast. Or let go.

Even one single match gives off light before it burns out. And that match has the power to light a lamp or start a fire.

Stoke the fires of your creativity. Light up your corner of the world.

April, 2017

FORTY-FOUR
FLINGING JOY IN THE FACE OF OPPRESSION

Fighting tyranny seems heroic. Larger than life. Sometimes it is. But mostly? Fighting tyranny requires both collective effort and individual change.

First, we confront the tyrants in our hearts and minds. Almost all of us have those bullying voices, trying to keep us small and afraid.

Second, we find ways to counter tyranny at every turn. The unjust actions. The brutal words.

Confronting tyranny is an act of hope.

Confronting tyranny is an invocation of a better world.

RIGHT NOW, *protestors in Atlanta, Georgia, are being charged with terrorism and racketeering because they have decided the only remaining urban forest in the state is more important than another training facility for militarized police.*

CHALLENGING tyranny begins when we examine our fears and prejudices.

We challenge tyranny by confronting our inner misogyny, racism, fatphobia, transphobia, xenophobia, and our fear of poverty and illness.

We challenge tyranny by embracing the power of flow and change.

We challenge tyranny by dancing in the light of the moon.

A COMRADE *I haven't seen in years just died. He lived a simple yet extraordinary life. Father Louie Vitale fed and clothed people. He gave them places to sleep.*

Father Louie also went up against the corrupt systems that forced these people into poverty in the first place. He was repeatedly arrested for disturbing the false peace that protects the status quo. He went up against warmongers, polluters, and weapons makers.

He challenged the status quo every day of his life, by simply living the way he saw fit.

WE CAN LIVE as we see fit, in our own power, and in our own time.

Tyranny is challenged by our thoughts that refuse to make enemies of our friends.

Tyranny is challenged by refusing to mark another person being as subhuman.

Tyranny is challenged when we question why eight people have more money and resources than eight million.

Tyranny is challenged when we insist that our communities are important, more important than the stockpiling of gold.

SOPHIE SCHOLL, *along with her brother and friends, drafted a series of pamphlets enjoining the German people to stand up against fascism. To not succumb to hatred. To not go along with the machine that ground too many bones to dust.*

They were executed for the simple act of distributing pamphlets. They were executed because words have the power to change hearts and minds.

Tyranny does not like that.

TYRANNY IS CHALLENGED with every kind word. Every refusal to back down. Every racist, sexist, queerphobic, or anti-trans statement challenged.

Tyranny is opposed with every garden planted and every resource shared. Tyranny is challenged with every anti-fascist sticker slapped on the back of a street sign. Tyranny is challenged when we remember we can take care of each other.

AT A RECENT CONCERT, *Janelle Monae enjoined us all to choose love, over and over, and to share pleasure. Because insisting on love and pleasure are direct challenges to tyranny.*

We must live, and live well.

WORDS CHALLENGE TYRANNY. Actions challenge tyranny. Emotions challenge tyranny. Art, music, and theater challenge tyranny. The stories we tell can either support or tear down tyranny.

We challenge tyranny when we allow ourselves to rest. We challenge tyranny when we revel in pleasure. We challenge tyranny when we insist on being alive, as we are.

Love and defiance challenge tyranny.

We can fling joy in the faces of those who would seek to oppress us.

BOOKS ARE BANNED. *Whole classes of human being are made illegal. Immigrants drown. Children are punished. Workers are exploited. The earth is ripped to pieces, sold off to the ones with the most money or the loudest shareholders.*

WE CHALLENGE tyranny when we examine our assumptions. We challenge tyranny when we refuse to call the cops on noisy neighbors. We challenge tyranny with every block party thrown, every cleanup organized, every fascist faced down in the bar or on the street.

We challenge tyranny with every union organized and every worker collective founded.

I'VE HAD *reviewers complain that my fantasy novels are too filled with politics. You know what that means? I was making visible things that they wanted to remain invisible. See, that's another way to challenge tyranny: to name things properly.*

TO NAME RACE, gender, economic class, and sexuality out loud is to challenge the tyranny of the ruling sects who want to keep us silent. When we are silent for too long, we become complicit in our own oppression and in the oppression of others.

Naming is a powerful magical act. Let us name ourselves and listen to the names of our communities.

CHARLIE CHAPLIN FOUGHT TYRANNY. *Audrey Hepburn fought tyranny. Josephine Baker fought tyranny. Tommy Smith and John Carlos fought tyranny. Ida B.*

Wells fought tyranny. Nelson Mandela fought tyranny. Dorothy Day fought tyranny. Marsha P. Johnson, Stormé deLarvarie, and Sylvia Rivera fought tyranny....

EVERYONE WHO FOUGHT tyranny in the past also worked to build something better. A place of art, and music, and movement. A place where their friends could be free.

Fighting tyranny is something we can do every single day.

It starts by noticing that the world is a beautiful, complex place. It starts by centering around love.

To fight tyranny is to say, "We are here, and we shall not comply with orders or actions that diminish us."

To fight tyranny is, to quote Emma Goldman, to insist upon *"freedom, the right to self-expression, everybody's right to beautiful, radiant things."*

Who's with me?

September, 2023

FORTY-FIVE

MARLEY'S HOT ON THE BOX

ON ART, JOY, AND REBELLION

I was singing Stevie Wonder's "Master Blaster," and a friend said, "I haven't thought about that song in years."

"I return to this song all the time," I replied.

Why? Because not only is Stevie Wonder a skilled songwriter and musician, "Master Blaster" encapsulates a vision of the world where enjoying life is a way to stand up to tyranny.

The story unfolds: It's hot out. There's a block party. Bob Marley is playing from someone's boom box. People are feeling good and looking good.

Oh, the world has problems, Stevie Wonder reminds us, and the folks in power want us to fight one another, but you know what? We're going to lift each other up, instead. We're going to enjoy each other's company.

The people in power cannot crush the spirit of community.

IN MY YOUTH, Rai music was popular. The bright sounds from Algeria came to the US in the 1980s, and I was told the music was "political." At first, I was confused.

"This is party music," I said. Ah, but that was part of the point. Little did I know at the time, the long history that led to the rise of Rai in the 1970s. And the songs were about social change, though I could not always hear it. The songs were about farmers, and working people, and struggle, and yes, about having a good time.

The Algerian government did not want people gathering. Fundamentalists did not want women singing. The people rebelled and did both. Rai was the music of resistance, and dancing, and enjoying life when the ruling regimes wanted to crush the spirit.

The spirit rose up and sang.

I'VE WRITTEN before about the way in which all art is political, depending on how you look at it. Who gets training? Who has access? Whose voices are predominant? Who makes the money?

These questions are embedded in the reigning social order. Anyone who bucks that system is considered political, or dangerous, or defanged by the brand of exceptionalism.

What characters are portrayed as good? What characters are portrayed as bad? What characters and voices are not included at all?

By now, we all know about Hollywood's "Middle Eastern" filter, that turns skies and cities a depressing orangey-brown to convey how terrible things are in that part of the world, how those places are filled with danger and deceit. We are aware of the ubiquitous maps of the world where the scale of the United States is completely disproportionate to any physical reality.

Those who redraw maps redraw our perception of the world. Mapmaking can become a form of oppression, or a form of rebellion and resistance. When we make our own maps, we can show each other the way.

And those people who ask why we have maps with borders rather than topography? Well, they may be called crackpots, or they may be called visionaries. Are they ever called realists?

You tell me.

KATHE KOLLWITZ DREW images of mothers protecting children. "The Seed Corn is Not For Grinding" was the message to warmongers and fascists.

NO Bonzo makes art and creates murals that remind us that we are all we have, and that collective action keeps us strong.

Keith Haring drew bright, childlike images in the midst of the worst of the AIDS crisis as a testament that his community was still there, despite the best attempts of the government to kill off every one of his friends.

Judith Jameson, Alvin Ailey, Leontyne Price, Nina

Simone...they all danced and sang both in celebration and resistance. They changed the world by doing it.

I'M WRITING a new novel series. It's another set of paranormal cozy mysteries, this time with corgis instead of a cat. The non-dog protagonists are two gay men.

Hmm... I thought. *These novels don't have the same social conscience of my other books. There isn't any explicit politics of resistance, like in my urban fantasy books. There's not even the emphasis on community action, like in my Seashell Cove cozies.*

Then I stopped myself.

I'm writing about two gay men living their lives. One of those men is trans and probably somewhere on the autism spectrum. Oh, and there's a ghost, too. A leather daddy named Adam. A former member of ACT UP who died at the height of the AIDS epidemic.

That alone is enough. That alone will be considered "political" in a time where being queer and trans is a dangerous thing. Where neurodivergence is feared. Where queer history is being whitewashed and diminished. People are killed for being queer or trans—especially Black trans women. Parents are moving their trans children across state lines to protect them. Many people's lives are hanging by a thread.

So, some cozy books about a trans gay man and his partner and two cute dogs, solving mysteries and living day to day?

That very celebration is rebellion. Is resistance. I

don't want it to be, but that's the world we live in now, isn't it?

In a society where my very existence is threatened, just living can be seen as a fight.

So, I might as well show up, and insist on my right to live and the rights of my friends and loved ones to thrive.

I'VE LONG SAID I write the world I want to live in. Whether that's nonfiction or fiction, it's all the same. As a society, we can choose how we live with one another, yet we repeatedly return to oppressing each other and poisoning this earth.

Stories, art, music, movies, dance...all of these are ways we hold out a hand to each other and insist, "You are not alone."

James Baldwin reminded us of that.

All forms of art and expression can become vehicles to say to the ruling powers, "You do not own us." And "There is a better way."

Through our creativity, we can throw a block party for each other, just like in Stevie Wonder's song. We can dance in the summer sun. Dancing won't make our problems go away, but it just might help us face them—feeling stronger and more joyful—tomorrow.

We can make art in solidarity with the world we build together.

We can slap stickers on the backs of street signs, leaving markers, blazing a trail.

We can choose to live, and live well, sharing what we

have in this crumbling society, in this amazing, beautiful world.

July, 2022

FORTY-SIX
INTERDEPENDENCE AND MUTUAL AID

Not one thing in our cosmos exists without impacting and being impacted by everything around it.

Recently, we dropped off a case of ready-to-eat vegetarian meal pouches at the Little Free Pantry in our neighborhood. Last time we did a drop-off, others were there, too, also dropping off supplies.

This time, I commented, "Oh, look. Someone else just dropped off some food. That's good!"

The person walked away, holding an empty sack that I assumed had been filled with food moments before.

I was wrong.

When I approached the pantry shelves, the only things on them were some sad radishes and one very mushy banana. The person walking away with the empty sack was a neighbor, hoping for food.

The person noticed us, and as we drove off, I saw them turn and head back. Hopefully they like Indian food, because that was what we left.

You wouldn't necessarily look at my neighborhood and think there was food insecurity here. But you never know. Times are hard for far too many of us.

That neighbor has likely come to rely on whatever food gets dropped at the little pantry, just as the crows, opossums, and songbirds rely on the bird bath in our backyard and the water bowls I fill out front.

That neighbor has likely come to rely on a food source, just as I rely on the trees to give off oxygen, and the bees and wasps to pollinate the plants, and the soldier flies to lay their larvae in the compost heap, breaking down vegetable scraps to feed the soil.

I've got friends who regularly feed people sleeping beneath freeway underpasses. I've got a comrade who repairs old electronics and gives them away. I've learned what kind of donations these friends and comrades can use, to pass things from our household—and from other, wealthier friends—to those who have greater need.

But Mutual Aid takes many forms:

There are people who tutor children or adults. There are small groups who volunteer to clean up yards and chop down dangerous trees and cut the logs into firewood for those who want or need it. There are folks who will step between victims and aggressors, breaking up attacks. There are others who offer free self-defense classes.

There are people offering counseling services at a discount, paid for by those who can afford a higher fee.

There are peer counselors, helping out each other.

There are people making art to keep us all inspired.

Everything in the cosmos shares what it has with everything else.

Everything except a few human beings who forget their interdependence, hoarding resources and exploiting others for their own gain. They tip the balance into danger and undermine the tenets of both interdependence and Mutual Aid.

Mutual Aid is predicated on acknowledgement of interdependence. Mutual Aid is not charity or philanthropy.

Mutual Aid is the rock-bottom, unshakeable knowledge that we are all in this life together and must share what skills and goods we have in order to survive and thrive.

I need help with my computer, and one person I know offers this. I'm happy to listen to a local activist who needs a sounding board. When I was at my sickest, people cared for me. When I am healthier, I care for others in turn.

This is not a one-to-one exchange. This is not quid pro quo. There is no keeping track or keeping score.

Mutual Aid is the flow of gifts throughout community. One day I need help, another day, you need help. One day I have something to offer. Another day you have something to offer. We all have skills and talents to share. You might give to one person and ask for help from yet another. And that is how it works. Mutual Aid builds functional, healthy, community systems.

We offer what we have and ask for what we need. We build a world—and a community—together.

Crows, squirrels, humans, beavers, wolves, gulls, plants, stars, planets, watersheds, clouds, and trees...there is nothing that exists outside these cycles of life that knit us together into one beautiful, radiant whole.

February, 2023

FORTY-SEVEN
MUTUAL AID IS COMMUNITY CARE

A big election happened in the US. Many people are devastated, reeling, angry, or fearful.

People fear that the already embattled protections trans and queer people have will be stripped away. People fear that already difficult to access healthcare will vanish. People fear that their friends, neighbors, or families will be rounded up and deported. People fear increased racism, misogyny, and violence. People fear that already tenuous environmental protections and regulations will be swept to sea or burned in the fires that decimate huge swathes of land.

People fear increased authoritarianism and fascism.

These people are not wrong.

Many people are waking up, once again, wondering how to help.

I'M A LEFTIST, an anarcho-socialist to be more precise. Or an anarcho-syndicalist if you're into political theory, which I'm not. Those of you who have read my novels—especially the Witches of Portland and Panther Chronicles series—or followed my writing for years may have known this. But a lot of people don't, because mostly, I just live my life.

Why am I telling you this? Because...

As a leftist, I never expect the government to do much to help the people. I trust no high-level politicians. I vote only under sufferance, and mostly to make what slight shifts are possible locally so the worst-off denizens of the city I live in aren't further burdened by the punishment of poverty and lack of resources. Sometimes I attend city council meetings.

Yes, things are likely to get very, very bad. And because I'm a leftist, my actions going forward won't be that different from my actions last week, or two years ago, or twenty. The election results didn't devastate me emotionally; rather, I started thinking of different ways we may need to organize in the future.

I'm less radical than some of my activist comrades and friends, and more radical than my liberal or progressive friends. My days of doing direct action may—or may not—be over, because of an autoimmune disorder and aftermath of a brain injury, plus, I'm pushing sixty now. And that's okay.

There's a place for all of us when it comes to community care.

Do I have concerns? Of course, I do. I'm queer and nonbinary in a queer partnership. I live communally. I have Black, Jewish, Muslim, Asian, Latine, and Indigenous—and trans, queer, poor, and disabled—comrades and friends. I'm neurodivergent and have invisible disabilities.

But my concerns don't lay me flat, rather, they point me to gaps in my thinking or organizing.

I'm not saying you shouldn't be grieving, or angry, or freaking out this week. I'm just explaining why I'm not: it's because I see the ways in which the world has always been this way and I feel prepared for action. I'm always prepared for, and engaging in, small, community-based actions, most of which I never talk about. Many of my friends are the same.

My hope with this essay is to offer a possible way forward for people unused to consistent community organizing.

THERE'S a common phrase among activists: "We keep us safe." Partially, this means people doing direct action band together in protection, but on a larger scale? "We keep us safe" means we don't rely on outside forces to foster and sustain community. We don't outsource our care.

Decades ago, when I worked full time in a soup kitchen, we didn't hire security guards. Instead, people like me were trained to de-escalate violence and break up fights, even those that involved weapons. We didn't rely on the government to feed people, we just did it ourselves. That's the sort of thing I'm talking about.

Before someone goes there: I'm not here to argue that government shouldn't provide healthcare, or regulate industry, or clean the water supply, or anything else. I wish it would. All I'm saying is, there is a lot more we can do together than we sometimes think.

There's an expansion on "We keep us safe" that is sometimes used as well: "We keep each other safe, so we can be dangerous together."

Some of us will be called upon to fight racism, misogyny, transphobia, homophobia, xenophobia, and outright fascism directly—in ways both large and small—at work, in school, in public washrooms, on the bus, or around the dinner table. Prepare for this in advance. Study bystander intervention skills. Train yourself to center internally, via various meditation or martial arts practices. Practice catch-phrases you can call upon under stress.

Remember: one person speaking up helps others speak up, too.

Stand up to racists. If a trans person needs to use a washroom, offer back up. Find out who is showing up to protect Drag Queen Story Hour. Take a breath and interrupt when a Black woman is being harassed on the street.

And if it comes to larger direct actions to protect immigrants or trans people, or confront police violence, or get vulnerable people to safety…? Study. Prepare. Get together with some trusted friends. Make a plan. Keep it secret.

All of this is part of community care.

There is a lot more I could say on this topic, but mostly today, I want to talk about another major form of community care: Mutual Aid. The term was coined by

Kropotkin in 1902, but Indigenous societies, worker cooperatives, and other groups have lived by these principles for centuries.

Mutual Aid is about cooperation and reciprocity. It is not charity or noblesse oblige. Mutual Aid is about mutual benefit. What helps you, helps me, and vice versa. We are all in this together.

Mutual Aid is a long-standing, leftist—but not only leftist—community building project. Mutual Aid is people sharing skills and resources.

Mutual Aid is part of how we keep us safe.

THAT'S GREAT, you might say, but how do we begin? Below are some practical ideas. Please read them all. Some may surprise you:

Get to know your neighbors if it is safe for you to do so. Share plants. Check on elders. Offer tools or other resources. Lend your skills to community projects. Chop and share firewood. Shovel snow. Set up a free pantry on your street. See if your disabled neighbor needs errands run while you're out. Buy some Plan B or Ella and let people know you have it. Do clinic defense. Give someone $10 toward medicine or food.

Pool money to buy a community generator so if the power goes out there is refrigeration for people's medicines and some perishable food to share. Figure out who has working vehicles with room to evacuate those who don't in case of a disaster. Connect those people.

In secret: connect someone fleeing abuse with someone who has a spare room.

Find ways to reach others outside of billionaire-owned social media sites. Get together with friends to make informational fliers or 'zines and drop them at coffee shops or post them on utility poles. Have a canning party. Teach sewing or self-defense. Share tools. Do research, or read to kids, or organize a community phone text tree...

All of this is what we call Mutual Aid.

Think about it: What might our community health look and feel like if we stopped framing things in terms of charity and began thinking in terms of justice? Mutual aid fosters greater social justice through community strength and survival.

What might our community health look and feel like if we stopped trying to get ahead just for ourselves and shared what we have?

The poorest people I know give away exponentially more, percentage-wise—in money, time, and resources—than the richest people I know. It is not that my richer friends aren't generous, it is because poor people know directly that community survival is the only way an individual survives, too.

STILL CONFUSED about where to begin?

Support larger Mutual Aid or community projects if you can. This is where you can look to social media. Local activist groups often have a presence there, even if most organizing is done via secure text, or in person. Whether or not you agree with them politically, Marxists and Anarchists are the ones doing consistent mutual aid, 365 days a year. Black women have a long track record of grass roots organizing. Indigenous people carry knowledge about reciprocity and resource sustainability.

Don't rush in like a stampeding bull, demanding a place at the table. Skirt around the edges for a while working on your own, smaller actions. Read. Listen. Learn. Then look for an opportunity to help. Where is there already community support for pregnant people, or elders? Is someone organizing a school lunch project? Does the coat drive need a well-designed flier? Does the Black or Indigenous run farm have a clean-up day? Is there an eyeglasses distribution bloc? Tech folks refurbishing old electronics? Do the anarchists spearheading disaster relief need a strong back, a truck, or some money or goods?

Is a friend getting rid of a heater, or air conditioner, or computer tablet, and is there a local group that redistributes goods to those who need them? I'm not talking about your neighborhood "buy nothing" group, though those have a place in the larger ecosystem. I'm talking about hooking up with groups or individuals who seek out those most in need who can least afford things like a refurbished laptop or quality air purifier.

Who is organizing jail support? Who is helping immigrants? Who is doing a clothing give away for trans or queer youth? Who has opened an emergency shelter? Who is making menstrual products and condoms available to teens? Who is planting a community garden?

Who is working with unhoused people to coordinate trash removal, or agitate for housing? Who is doing co-counseling training or offering vetted herbal health information?

There are likely people doing all of the above somewhere near you. But really? The answer to any of those questions could be you and some of your friends.

Also, how accessible are community gatherings or meetings? Are people wearing masks so immunocompromised people feel welcome? Is there wheelchair access? A scent-free space? A quiet corner? An ASL interpreter? Children's activities? Accessibility is part of community care as well.

Mutual Aid. We've always needed it. A lot of our ancestors did it naturally, until suburbs, freeways, and the insistence on the primacy of the nuclear family eroded the systems that were keys to our survival and well-being.

But it is never too late to try. It is never too late to build systems of care.

Remember, it's the small stuff—done with consistency—that provides a platform for true community well-being. Stop looking for a big fix or a heroic act. Just keep finding ways to show up.

And in the midst of it all? Don't forget to sing. To dance. To make and share art.

Don't forget that love is the bedrock of Mutual Aid. Let's show up for what we love.

November, 2024

FORTY-EIGHT
A HOME INSIDE EACH HEART

"We're all just walking each other home." — Ram Dass

Throughout my life, from around age thirteen on, I've cycled into and out of various forms of activism. During the longest stretches, I've returned again and again to the basics of feeding people and helping out where I can, while working on long-term culture change.

Why? First, I believe in people more than institutions. Yes, I know that institutions are made up of people, but they also take on a life and spirit of their own. As an anarcho-socialist, the actions of government have never sat quite right with me, though I've engaged with elected government under sufferance, off and on.

Second, the direct political engagement that felt available to me also felt frustrating in the long run. Massive marches. Blockades. City council meetings. The multiple times I've been arrested. What was the result? Did the needle actually move? Not against war and support for war, unfortunately. The US government never seemed to care, no matter how many of us were in the streets or how many risked arrest. Unless there were enough of us to clog the courts, we were fleas on the back of the government's dog.

And there are always too many others who never risked arrest but were put behind bars simply for existing in their skin, giving lie to the relative privilege of my own actions.

More targeted actions—those blockades or other events that included education about the bloodstained hands of multinational corporations, for example—did feel worthwhile to me. Supporting Occupy Wall Street in Oakland and Occupy ICE in Portland felt worthwhile to me. Standing with the families of loved ones killed by police is always worth my time. Sending eSIMs or money to people trying to survive in unconscionable conditions is one small act that has immediate positive impact.

In other words, I haven't given up. I hope I never will.

With that said, these days as tech companies exploit children and use up community water supplies to keep their generative AI models running, when other companies buy the rest of the water to sell it back to us, when people living on the street because of lack of mental health services and a laughable minimum wage have all of their possessions repeatedly stolen by government agencies, when people's bodies are consistently policed, when Indigenous people are still being disappeared and queer people murdered, arms shipped and torture upheld, when the US Supreme Court rules that an individual can kill scores of others in minutes because the rights of guns are more important than people, when the global south has all its riches stolen and bears the brunt of climate change caused by a few in the north.... What of all of that?

I admit we are currently in a complete, escalating societal collapse and that the people who have claimed power over the rest of us don't seem to care. The glorification of material wealth has spawned billionaire oligarchs with politicians in their pockets. The rest of us are one medical disaster or one slender paycheck away from losing everything.

Living under a collapsing empire on a gasping planet is not safe or pleasant for far too many.

So, what do I do? What do we do?

I return, once again, to helping where I can. To making sure people have food. To hopefully easing the hearts of those who read my books, watch my videos, or see a picture I snapped of a roadside flower.

It never feels like enough, but in this war of too many fronts, it is still all that I have. Culture change happens when we can imagine something better for each other and ourselves.

As I've said hundreds of times: do what you can, when you can, where you can.

We can uplift each other's voices. We can buy birth control and pass it on. We can escort people into clinics. We can offer safe spaces for queer youth. We can dismantle the machinery that rips apart precious habitats. We can deliver fuel to Indigenous elders. We can drop jugs of water in the desert for those crossing from danger. We can agitate for housing. We can support small farming cooperatives and worker-owned collectives. We can redistribute goods. We can share our skills and talents. We can speak truth to power.

We can dismantle the human propensity toward greed, violence, and oppression one kindness at a time. To do otherwise is to give in to despair.

I am neither ready nor willing to pick up the guns of revolution. Perhaps this is cowardice on my part, or a sense of being tired. Or perhaps this is my way of saying that freedom won by violence begets more violence still. Or maybe, as some other people say, we need both those who are willing to fight a revolution, and those who are able to offer succor and aid to the ones most affected by the war.

I don't have an answer for that. All I know is: nothing is inevitable, even when it feels that way.

Years ago, while teaching at a conference, someone asked what the use of all this striving was. My response was that if we do not work together toward evolution, we foster devolution.

I do not want to foster devolution.

So, I'll continue to offer what hope, vision, and comfort I can, through my writing and my art. I'll support community as best I can, through a series of small, ongoing actions.

A belief in community is important, both locally and

globally, because we are all we have. We have to keep each other alive to greet another day.

For, as Ram Dass said, we are all just walking each other home.

And home is held inside each heart, if we allow it to be. If we allow it to grow. Together.

June, 2024

FORTY-NINE
A WALK IN SOFT JUNE RAIN

After working inside all day long, I've finally made it out for a walk. I'm wearing a T-shirt, jeans, and boots, and it's raining.

Droplets kiss my skin and spatter on my glasses. It feels beautiful. It feels good.

It reminds me that I am alive. There is more to life than business and books, more even than the weight and worries of the world: there are wild roses, and bleating baby goats—yes, even in this city neighborhood—and trees reaching for the rain. There is damp soil and a squirrel eating a grape on a tree stump.

I breathe in. I breathe out. I'm doing for myself what I did for a client earlier today. My client needed a chance to simply sit and breathe awhile, so after talking, that's what we did. I guided them through a brief meditation, and hoped it was of help.

But my body needed movement, and my mind needed to slow down. To re-center. So, I walk in the rain and I run my hands over the needles of a rosemary bush, cupping my palms in front of my face, inhaling the fragrance to clear my mind. Walking helps both my body and my mind.

Walking eases my heart from the pain of the world.

A crow calls to its mate. Flowers grow past fence posts. On a front stoop, a man in work boots and a ball cap has an after-work cigarette. He waves and smiles in greeting. I do the same, and continue walking down the city sidewalk.

I am happy to be alive. Happy to feel the kiss of water. Happy for a cloudy June afternoon in Portland, Oregon.

I'm happy now, to be sharing this moment with you.

What moments keep you going? What do you enjoy? What feels sacred to you?

In the midst of the hustle, and the worry, and the pain, how often do you pause to breathe and feel moisture on your skin? How often do you lift your face to the sky and insist to the world: "Today I am alive, and I will keep living for as long as it takes."

I breathe that in, too. And I say it again:

"Today, I am alive. And I will keep on living for as long as it takes."

Keep breathing, friends. And enjoy what moments of deliciousness you can.

June, 2024

FIFTY
WE ACT TO LOVE THIS WORLD

We act because we are in love. In love with a world in pain. In love with a world so bright, so dark, so hideous, so gorgeous, so alive.

We act because love thrums through our veins, beating out the cadence life, life, life.

And we return to life, even amid death and terror.

We are furious. And sometimes afraid. And some days we want to give up...

But our hearts still beat, and air still whispers through our lungs.

Love is all we have some days, even if we think love has forgotten our names.

We act, because we are in love. We are in love with brown bodies and bright minds, with the possibility that lights up children's faces, and the whole, glorious array of human beings, everywhere.

We are in love with ocean and mountain. We are in love with sun and rain, concrete and sky.

We act, because we love.

And the moment love is extinguished?

The future we envision dies.

So, bring your rage, your disappointment, your depression, your pain, your joy, your creative spark, your tear, your lack of knowing. Bring it all.

Let us build mutuality and aid. Let us build beauty and care. Let us build food and shelter. Let us build equity, and justice, and more love.

Today is a day to rise

Today is a day to raise your fist (if you can) and shout out to the world:

"I am in love with you! I am with you! Until the end!"

June, 2018

RESOURCES

Some Tips for Safer Organizing

This first portion is for those who might need to engage in activities the state will decree as illegal. It is by no means exhaustive, but should give you a start. Books and other resources are below this section.

Electronic security

- Use encryption for all communication, not just organizing
    - Signal for text messages and phone calls: WhisperSystems.org
    - Visit the Electronic Frontier Foundation ssd.eff.org for more electronic security information.
    - Never use Facebook, Gmail, Threads, or

any social media or open email for sensitive organizing

- Use strong passwords & a password manager
- Use a password—best six-digit or longer—to lock your phone or tablet (police can get a court order to force you to use any biometric lock, like a fingerprint or face scan)

Personal Preparation

- Learn how to deal with tear gas, pepper spray, and LRAD, and have the necessary supplies pre-packed. Clean water, face masks, ear plugs, water mixed with plain milk of magnesia...
- Buy or make a foil or anti-static, RFID protection bag to hide your cellphone from monitoring when you don't need it connected. Or better yet, leave your phone at home. Your phone is a physical tracker.
- Get phone numbers for the local Lawyers Guild (or the National Lawyers Guild, or ACLU) and have them with you; write these on your body if going to an action.
- Take self-defense classes if you can, to improve your physical confidence: train your emotions and psyche.
- Do basic street medic training if that is of interest, and put together a medic kit. There

are many info resources online. Use private search.

- Wear Black Bloc, which means full-coverage black, neutral clothing.
- Always arrive and leave with a buddy.

Coordination Preparation

- Plan (encrypted!) phone trees—Latine activists in the '90s could fill a plaza within a couple of hours just with phone trees
- Meet in person

When Meeting in Person

Use these rules for any meetings that require security, like planning direct action or safety organizing for at-risk communities:

- Make sure you trust all the people you are in the room with
- Switch up meeting locations regularly
- Decide on your group's security protocols in advance
- Don't discuss plans for actions where you can be overheard: bars, backyards, etc.
- Prevent eavesdropping through computers and phones

1. Power everything down (with batteries out if possible)
2. Keep them out of the room entirely
3. Put phones in a metal bowl or box as a Faraday cage. Microwaves work in a pinch

- Decide on message codes in person first for use in text and email. For example...
- Communicating about plans: "We're going to visit Grandma"
- Arrest risk level: "I'm bringing roses," meaning down with getting arrested... "Daffodils are awesome," meaning you don't want to risk arrest but can deal with it... "I prefer tulips," meaning you cannot risk arrest at all. People often use variations on red, yellow, and green to denote risk ability. Make your own code.
- Have some members of the group as a support team to do things like call the National Lawyers Guild, make sure your stuff is safe, meet you at jail, monitor police scanners, or bring snacks or water during actions if needed
- If appropriate to the action, have an in-house media person who can get the word out during or after the action

Make sure the most impacted voices are heard, and in leadership if possible.

Take care of your community.

Take care of yourself.

Books, Zines, and Other Resources:

Seek out locally or online:

- Basic Bystander Intervention Training
- Basic De-escalation Training
- Street Medic Training and Supplies

Research locally or online:

- Immigrants' Rights Organizations
- Trans Rights Organizations
- LGBTQ+ Rights Organizations
- Black Led Organizations
- Latine Led Organizations

Books, Articles, and Zines:

- *40 Ways to Fight Fascists* by Spencer Sunshine
- *Joyful Militancy: Building Thriving Resistance in Toxic Times* by carla bergman and Nick Montgomery
- *Emergent Strategy* by adrienne maree brown
- *So You Want to Talk About Race* by Ijeoma Oluo
- *The Fire Next Time* by James Baldwin

- *The New Jim Crow* by Michelle Alexander
- *The 5 Methods of Divestment and Weaponization of White Power and Privilege* by Community Ready Corp (for Allies and Accomplices) crc4sd.org
- *Where Do We Go from Here: Chaos or Community?* By Dr. Martin Luther King Jr.

Small Publishers with Worthy Books:

- AK Press
- Daraja Press
- Microcosm Publishing

Some Websites to Search For:

- Community Ready Corp for Safety and Defense
- Electronic Frontier Foundation
- Neighborhood Anarchist Collective
- Mutual Aid Disaster Relief
- Mutual Aid Hub
- The Commons Library

Thank you to my Kickstarter backers, who made this updated edition possible.
Deep thanks again to my Patreon supporters. These essays would not have been written without you all.

Also thanks to Jack for his input on the updated manuscript and Dayle for editing.

If you enjoyed this book, please consider telling a friend, or leaving a review.
Many thanks!

Also, Thorn has a weekly newsletter if you want to keep in touch. Visit thorncoyle.com for more information.

ALSO BY T. THORN COYLE

FICTION

Seashell Cove Paranormal Cozy Mysteries

Bookshop Witch

Haunted Witch

Tarot Witch

Running Witch

Hallows Witch

Solstice Witch

The Pride Street Paranormal Cozy Mysteries

Sushi Scandal

Flower Frenzy

Muffin Murder

Hairspray Horror

The Mouse Thief

Mouse's Folly

Mouse's Fight

The Witches of Portland (complete)

By Earth

By Flame

By Wind

By Sea

By Moon

By Sun

By Dusk

By Dark

By Witch's Mark

The Panther Chronicles (Complete)

To Raise a Clenched Fist to the Sky

To Wrest Our Bodies From the Fire

To Drown This Fury in the Sea

To Stand With Power on This Ground

The Steel Clan Saga

We Seek No Kings

We Heed No Laws

We Ride at Night

Short Story Collections

A Hint of Faery

A Touch of Faery

A Spark of Magic

A Flame for Yuletide

A Hope for Winter

A Time for Magic

A Speculation of Stars

A Speculation of Hope

A Speculation of Time

Risk It All: Queer Stories of Love, Suspense, And Daring

Thresholds: Queer Stories of Love, Suspense, And Daring

Ghost Talker

Cats and Other Creatures

NON-FICTION

You are the Spell

Sigil Magic for Writers, Artists, & Other Creatives

Crafting a Daily Practice

Resistance Matters

Evolutionary Witchcraft

Kissing the Limitless

Make Magic of Your Life

The MidList Indie Author Mindset

ABOUT THE AUTHOR

T. Thorn Coyle worked in many strange and diverse occupations before settling in to write books full time.

Author of the *Seashell Cove Paranormal Mystery* series, the *Pride Street Paranormal Cozy Mysteries, The Steel Clan Saga, The Witches of Portland, The Mouse Thief Adventures*, and *The Panther Chronicles*, Thorn's multiple non-fiction books include *Sigil Magic for Writers, Artists & Other Creatives, Kissing the Limitless, Make Magic of Your Life,* and *Evolutionary Witchcraft*. Thorn's work also appears in many anthologies, magazines, and collections.

An interloper to the Pacific Northwest U.S., Thorn drinks a lot of tea, pays proper tribute to the neighborhood cats, and talks to crows, squirrels, and trees.

Connect with Thorn:
www.thorncoyle.com

www.ingramcontent.com/pod-product-compliance
Lightning Source LLC
Chambersburg PA
CBHW070057030426
42335CB00016B/1918

* 9 7 8 1 9 4 6 4 7 6 5 6 2 *